A Wag's as Good as a Smile

A Wag's as Good as a Smile

Billy Roberts

BOOKS

Winchester, UK
Washington, USA

First published by Sixth Books, 2012
Sixth Books is an imprint of John Hunt Publishing Ltd., Laurel House, Station Approach,
Alresford, Hants, SO24 9JH, UK
office1@o-books.net
www.o-books.com

For distributor details and how to order please visit the 'Ordering' section on our website.

Text copyright: Billy Roberts 2011

ISBN: 978 1 78099 164 1

A CIP catalogue record for this book is available from the British Library.

Design: Stuart Davies

Printed and bound by CPI Group (UK) Ltd, Croydon, CR0 4YY
Printed in the USA by Edwards Brothers Malloy

We operate a distinctive and ethical publishing philosophy in all
areas of our business, from our global network of authors to
production and worldwide distribution.

CONTENTS

INTRODUCTION

Over the last 20 years or so a great deal has been written about the psychic powers of animals but, as far as I am aware, very little has been mentioned about the Healing Powers which animals undoubtedly possess. The therapeutic value of having a pet of any kind around the home is widely accepted today, and this theory has now extended to the practice of taking dogs to visit the elderly and the infirm in hospices, rest homes and hospitals, in the belief that *'A pat a day keeps the doctor away.'*

P.A.T dogs (Pets As Therapy) are proving extremely beneficial particularly in encouraging the recovery and rehabilitation of severely depressed patients, or those who have simply given up the will to live. In such cases, where perhaps the patient has ceased to communicate with those around them, the introduction of a friendly, gentle dog into the environment has often been instrumental in renewing the patient's interest in life. Those confined to nursing homes for the elderly also appear to derive benefit from their P.A.T dogs, and each canine visit is eagerly awaited.

There is most certainly more at work here than the simple physical contact between human and animal. Many people accept that there is a metaphysical aspect to the therapeutic value of their pet, and that this transcends the creature's physical, cuddly presence.

Of course some animals are far from cuddly, but even they are still able to create an atmosphere of healing where there is sickness and depression. One only has to consider, for example, the invaluable work done today with dolphins and the incredible way they affect children suffering with autism and other disabilities to appreciate just how special they really are, particularly in the field of healing. It almost seems as though the dolphins know exactly what they are doing, as they swim and play with the children brought sometimes great distances especially to see them. And perhaps this is not so very far from the truth.

Some people however would appear to be completely untouched by the healing powers of animals. This would seem to be the case particularly when a person is not too fond of any kind of animal.

Some sort of emotional contact has to be established between human and animal before the healing process really commences. However, the initiation of the healing process can be spontaneous and can take effect on the very first encounter, so it is therefore not necessarily dependent upon a long relationship. Taking time to stroke and speak to a friendly dog on the high street may be all that is needed to bring you relief from that niggling headache, or perhaps to lift that dark cloud of depression hanging over you, or to calm those taut nerves brought about by a stressful day. You have probably never put two and two together, and it has almost certainly never crossed your mind that the sudden disappearance of that awful headache had anything at all to do with that lovely old dog you patted in the Post Office.

However, physical contact is not a prerequisite to receiving healing from an animal nor, I must add, is the ability to discharge healing confined to dogs alone. On the contrary, cats, birds, and many other species of animals have a pronounced healing effect upon the human organism. Nor is this healing force confined to domestic pets, for many wild animals too contribute to this healing atmosphere which is so necessary for man's spiritual, mental and emotional equilibrium. I will go as far as to say with certainty that man could not exist on a planet devoid of animals, for the Animal Kingdom contributes far more to the spiritual evolution of mankind than we know or are able to understand.

A leisurely stroll through the tranquillity of secluded woodland is most certainly therapeutic in itself, but the accompaniment of birds whistling and singing along our way most definitely introduces some other, more subtle, vibratory sensations to the whole experience. These vibrations have a profound effect upon both the mind and the emotions. I am not talking here about a simple experience of the auditory senses. This pleasant phenomenon goes far beyond that. For the musical harmonies of birds singing in the countryside creates a healing veil of tranquillity which most definitely produces some sort of chemical change in the human brain.

Animals, like people, have a 'Psychic Profile'. There is far more to an animal than meets the purely physical eye.

Their personalities and characters also appear to be influenced by their astrological status, in much the same way as people. However, in the Animal Kingdom this influence is much more pronounced. For example, Capricorn and Cancer people nearly always possess an inherent desire to care for others, and they are very often attracted to some sort of caring profession as a result.

In the Animal Kingdom this emotion seems to be much more pronounced, and creatures born under these astrological signs create and release extremely vibrant healing forces into the surrounding environment. Of course this ability to discharge healing vibrations is far stronger in the creatures that interact with humans, such as family pets, as opposed to the wild animal.

In my exploration of the whole concept of the healing powers of animals I have come across many examples of the way in which humans have been positively altered, in one way or another, by this power. In my studies alone of the way animals have affected humans, it would be impossible to attribute every account to simple coincidence.

A journalist working for a major North of England newspaper told me about a pussycat she had adopted from an animal rescue centre. The middle-aged feline had obviously been badly treated, and when Felicity Newsone acquired him he was in a sorry state and greatly in need of some love and kindness. The pussycat showed his mistrust of humans by being subdued and refusing to meow or purr. Felicity tried to win her feline friend's confidence by holding the furry creature close to her face. She would then go through the process of breathing softly onto the pussycat's face in an effort to encourage and relax him. The warmth of the breath alone is usually sufficient to make the hardest of pussycats purr. However, this pitiful mite appeared to be completely silent and unaffected by the treatment. Felicity applied this therapy a couple of times a day seemingly without any great success. The little creature had obviously been traumatised, and Felicity knew that a great deal of love and patience would be needed. As a cat lover she was willing to do almost anything to make her feline companion happy and know he was loved and in safe hands. The weeks passed by and there seemed to be absolutely no response from the little creature. But then Felicity thought she could hear something and held her head close to her little friend. To her amazement she could hear the unmistakable sound of a purr. Although it was extremely faint and scarcely audible, it was most definitely a purr. Little Samson was beginning to trust again, and the healing process had begun to take place. Although it took some time Felicity's patience and love helped to heal and encourage little Samson back to good health, and today his purr is just as loud as any other healthy pussycat's. There is no doubt about it when Samson came into Felicity Newson's life he definitely fell on his paws. Although this story illustrates how the love of a human can greatly affect the healing process when a little creature has been injured, it is also indicative of the trust our pets place in us. Our pets are most certainly at our mercy, and do not have any control whatsoever over our impulsive actions. When a dog or cat finds itself living in a house bereft of love, it very often makes an asserted effort to win the affection of at least one member of the family. When all the little creature's efforts fail it very often falls into a psychological decline and becomes very sad. This, amazingly, is the creature's last asserted effort to access the emotions of those in the household, and it usually succeeds.

In this so called modern age of science and technology, there is very little doubt that our lives are becoming more and more stressful, and we seem to have very little time to relax and recover our natural energies. However, the medical world is now telling us that having either a dog or cat in the home actually promotes serenity and calmness and even aids recovery from illness. There is no doubt about it that a home bereft of animals has a completely different feeling than the home with a furry presence. In fact, it is often said that those who completely disregard animals secretly have a dislike of people. Some researchers have suggested that a dislike of animals is sometimes a symptom of emotional problems and can represent someone who is moody and quite volatile. Although this is not always the case, generally speaking those who love animals are far more sensitive than those who do not. Living with a pet has, in fact, been equated with having a mental pressure cooker in the home. It has been medically proven that being around dogs and cats does lower blood pressure and calms taught nerves. It is now known that having a pet actually eases the debilitating discomfort of back pain and even alleviates the misery of migraine. Tests have in fact been done in America, Britain and Russia on the way in which dogs affect the human psyche. It was concluded that in 8 out of 10 cases of those suffering with long-term depression recovery was far quicker when they lived with a loving canine than those who did not. Furthermore, it was shown that children brought up in an animal orientated home were calmer and suffered fewer anxiety problems in later life than those who had had no contact with animals during their childhood. Children brought up without a pet are even more aggressive in later life than the children brought up with animals. In fact, dogs are now being used to detect certain types of skin cancers in humans. This extraordinary canine skill is being employed by an American Dermatologist by the name of

Armond Cognetta. This specialised canine diagnostic practise is performed by a Schnauzer called 'George' and a Golden Labrador called 'Breeze' whose combined success rate is extremely high. Of course, dogs are now being trained to aid the disabled or infirm in many different ways. In fact, the P.A.T Dog (Pets As Therapy) has become extremely popular over the last decade or so, and it is now being realised that our canine friends are far more important to our well-being and emotional equilibrium than we ever imagined. One quadriplegic man in America lives his life with a small monkey who appears to know everything he is thinking. The man's tiny friend tidies the home, fetches food from the fridge, and even helps to feed her disabled master. Although some animal activists protested very strongly at the little creature's exploitation, it was in fact shown that the disabled man's little helper only did as much as she wanted to. When she'd had enough she simply went into the little house he had had made for her, and closed the door until she was ready to continue her chores. It is quite clear really that the individual souls that collectively make up the entire animal kingdom most certainly represent an extremely Divine Power that mankind cannot in any way comprehend at this stage of evolution. It is my personal opinion that we could not survive on a planet bereft of animals, and *they* most certainly contribute far more than we realise to man's spiritual, emotional and psychological equilibrium.

When one is depressed or perhaps just feeling sorry for one's self, there is no greater tonic than being greeted by the family dog wagging his or her tail. In fact, it is very difficult to ignore this kind of greeting, particularly when the little furry creature puts so much effort into it. A great deal of research has been done into the effects our pets have upon us and how their presence in the home affects our minds. Anyone who has a close relationship with his or her canine lodger will know only too well what I am talking about when I say that our pet often puts so much effort into transmitting their love to us. Research done in both America and Russia has shown that our pets contribute far more to our well being than just a warm, furry presence. Both dogs and cats release a subtle energy into the atmosphere that somehow has a remarkable effect upon the human brain. Not only is our pet able to calm our stressed and anxious mind, but he or she can somehow ease our physical pains by mysteriously aiding the release of endorphins in the brain, the body's natural pain killers. Although animal healing appears to be far more effective on animal lovers, it is by no means restricted to them.

Over recent years ferrets have been found to affect some sort of healing process in children. These playful creatures somehow interact well with children and have the unusual ability to encourage the healing process in those suffering with autism and other psychologically debilitating disorders. As with dogs and cats the ferret is also able to precipitate the release of endorphins and other chemicals in the brain, thus encouraging feelings of well-being. Research carried out with ferrets in controlled circumstances has been extremely positive, and the effect they have on disabled children has proved quite remarkable.

Although all animals possess some sort of metaphysical power, to some greater or lesser degree, in this book we shall be concerned primarily with domestic dogs and cats, as they are closer to us humans than any other animal. Hopefully, when we have concluded our exploration of their healing powers, we shall have discovered a whole new meaning to the old saying *'A man's best friend is his dog.'*

Author's note: There are times within the pages of this book where, in order to facilitate the flow of the text, I have been forced to refer to an animal as 'it'. I know that you, the reader, will forgive me.

CHAPTER ONE

THE HEALING NATURE

It is all too easy to dismiss the healing abilities of animals, particularly when one is not too fond of them. Nonetheless, the truth is that more and more evidence is being presented to us today to substantiate the numerous claims that the presence of a furry creature in the home is good for the health of the whole family. In fact, it has now been scientifically proven that dogs and cats are beneficial to the health and that they do have a profound effect upon both the body and mind. I am quite certain that most people will agree that when we are feeling a little sad and insecure, the warmth of our dog or cat is extremely reassuring and nearly always makes us feel a little better. Science is now telling us that this reassurance is not simply the result of warm fur against the skin. On the contrary, once we have allowed a dog or cat to interact into our family life, it usually discharges an extremely powerful force into the subtle atmosphere. This force can be scientifically measured and its effect upon the mind registered and monitored.

Over the past decade various studies have been made upon the effects animals have upon humans. The results of these studies show that those children who have been brought up with either a dog or cat are much more evenly tempered, and more emotionally and psychologically grounded in later life than those who have not. A high percentage of children brought up without a pet tended to be more aggressive in later life and often showed very little regard for animals. However, it must be said that this is not always the case, as a child may want a pet but may have been denied this by its parents.

It has always been argued that to be too passionate over

animals can also affect one's emotions and whole psychology adversely. In fact, those who dedicate their lives to fighting for the rights of animals often tend to live very unconventionally and occasionally choose to isolate themselves from the rest of society. A prime example is the French film actress Bridget Bardot who has become a recluse and now devotes her life entirely to animals.

It has always been my personal opinion that those who do not like animals at all lack something emotionally and very often appear cold; in fact, it was once said that those who do not like animals do not like people. Although this is not always the case, those who feel warm and loving towards other species are often more loving towards their own.

Cats and dogs exert great control over their owners and have an almost hypnotic effect upon them. For example, I am quite certain that every dog owner reading this book has had the experience of sitting comfortably in front of the fire on a chilly autumn evening, when suddenly the thought 'What about Lucky's walkies' sprang into their mind, quickly followed by overwhelming feelings of guilt. Try as you might, you simply cannot banish the thoughts from your mind and, as the minutes pass, the guilty feeling begins to irritate you. More often than not you give in to it, with thoughts such as 'Half an hour in the fresh air will do me the world of good,' or 'It's only fair to the little fellow.' So you stand up and call, 'Come on then, walkies!' Oddly enough, 99 times out of 100, your little dog is already at the door, waiting to go.

You may think, as most people would, that the little creature has 'picked up' its master's thoughts telepathically – but you would be very wrong. For there is no doubt that the process of telepathy – that is mind-to-mind communication – is always in operation between pet and its master, but more often than not, it is your pet who places the idea in your mind, and not the other way round!

Although dogs and cats are constantly 'tuned into' the collective minds of the family and therefore are able to exert a powerful control over the entire household, they usually single out one particular member with whom they feel a special bond and whom they know they can influence more. However, they do know instantly when a member of the family is unwell or even when the family is going on holiday.

Animals and people tend to think in pictures. However, because man has evolved speech as a mode of communication, he tends to be under the assumption that he thinks with words – he does not! If I ask you to think of an elephant it is not the word *'elephant'* you see in your mind, but the picture of an elephant. This is processed at an incredible speed and then converted into the word. Animals do not have the same mental processing system, as their method of communication is far simpler and much quicker. They mentally transmit a series of pictures of what exactly they wish to say. Because of the rapidity of their thought transmission, animals are able to *know* what you are thinking long before your thoughts manifest as words.

So, the telepathic 'traffic' is not all one way, and although your dog is quite capable of *receiving* your mental intentions telepathically, it is also perfectly able to psychically *convey* to you its own desires and wishes. So to come back to that initial cold autumn evening, your sudden decision to take your dog for a walk was in fact *sent* to you by your furry little friend (or maybe not so little) in subtle telepathic waves. Lucky was indeed one step ahead of you.

Although all animals possess healing properties in one form or another, it is the pets we live with who possess the greatest and most effective healing powers. Once a pet has established itself in the family environment, and is absolutely certain that it approves of everyone, it then sets about creating its own healing atmosphere. This is perhaps the primary reason why a home bereft of animals is somehow not quite the same as one which possesses a furry presence. I am not talking about the sometimes pungent aromas, so familiar to all dog and cat owners, which those who do not have animals find most unpleasant. Nor am I talking about discarded chews or a carpet of broken dog biscuits underfoot – commonplace things to pet owners. But rather there is another, more subtle force pervading the home of an animal keeper, and it is one that is immediately identifiable by another pet owner.

Those of you who share your homes with a dog or cat will understand exactly what I am referring to when I say, should your pet be absent from the home for even a short while, you are able to 'feel' their absence in the subtle atmosphere of the house. There is an identifiable 'emptiness' in the atmosphere, which most of us find disquieting and even upsetting. It is almost as though animal lovers belong to some exclusive secret society.

There is very little doubt that animals do exert an extraordinary psychological hold on us and are able to aid our recovery from illness. I am convinced too, that we do not choose our pets. On the contrary, they choose us by consciously, telepathically drawing us towards them. The very suggestion of this would no doubt be dismissed completely by the person who has a dislike of animals. Nonetheless, this is the belief of many animal lovers.

Once our pets have fully established themselves in the family environment, and the subtle atmosphere has been well and truly created, they then begin to attune themselves to each and every person in the household. Although a pet usually responds more to one particular person in the house (becoming known as either the man's or the woman's pet) the animal itself *homes-in* on the whole family, weaving its mantle of authority over the entire household. Once a pet has been accepted as one of the family, life is never the same again.

To someone who absolutely loves dogs there is absolutely nothing in the world like the cuddle of this warm, loving creature. There is definitely an exchange of energies during such contact that has an incredible calming effect upon the human mind. However, this calming process is most certainly not restricted to physical contact. A lover of animals also experiences great delight in watching animals relaxing or playing. Healing of some sort is always experienced through any degree of mental interaction with animals. This healing process is not confined to animal lovers, for whether they are aware of it or not, people who do not particularly like animals are also affected by the healing created by animals.

In my study of the whole subject of animal healing, I have found that – where the degree and type of healing is concerned – there is a marked difference from animal to animal. Some dogs appear to have a remarkable effect upon illnesses associated with the nerves and emotions, whilst others appear to be extremely beneficial in aiding general recovery after illness. Whilst the healing abilities of dogs usually has nothing whatsoever to do with size or breed, the bigger, more fluffier dogs generally have a holistic effect upon the person, and have a profound effect upon the body and the mind thus promoting the self-healing process.

The healing force is not transmitted through any one part of a dog's body, but is somehow created by the whole personality, aura and physical presence. Therefore the healing process is not dependent upon touch (although contact facilitates the healing process more efficiently) but merely being in the presence of some creatures for a length of time is really all that is needed. Evidence of this is seen when dogs are taken into homes for the elderly and infirm. In the presence of a canine visitor improvement is often seen in overall appearance and behaviour of the person. The P.A.T dog (Pets As Therapy) scheme has pioneered this discovery and rests on the very premise that elderly and infirm patients benefit from the company of dogs; because the results are extremely positive, the concept of P.A.T dogs has been introduced as an alternative approach to the more traditional therapies. It does not really matter whether the recipient of healing likes dogs or not, they can still be affected. Dogs with the more gentle temperaments appear to have the most effective healing abilities and the healing process is most certainly helped a great deal when the dog has a pleasant disposition.

Although sceptics (and there many) would say that our pets transmit this healing force – if there is one – unconsciously, I am not convinced that this is always the case. I would even go as far as to say that some dog and cat healers are totally aware of what they are doing, particularly when a close, loving relationship has been formed between them and their owner.

The P.A.T dogs will be covered at various lengths all through this book.

CHAPTER TWO

SCIENTIFIC FACTS

Research done in Russia, America, France and Britain has proved conclusively that having some sort of a pet is most definitely good for the health. In fact, children brought up with animals are, 99 times out of 100, calmer with more even temperaments. Those brought up with a dog as a pet seem to be less stressed and far more patient in later life, and most certainly less aggressive. In experiments done with patients suffering from Alzheimers it was found that once he or she had been introduced to a friendly canine, within 30 minutes they became less anxious, calmer and more coherent. The same experiments showed that elderly patients became relaxed and felt more secure in the company of either a cat or dog. Once a strong relationship had been formed, he or she had a much brighter outlook and became more positive as a consequence. In one young offenders prison in America Labradors and Border Collies were introduced to ten of the inmates, whose persistent offending and anti-social behaviour meant that their future looked quite bleak. After eight weeks of sharing their lives with the friendly canines nine out of the ten inmates changed remarkably. Each one appeared to express emotions and sides to their natures they had never shown before. The inmate who rejected the experiment did so because it was thought that he was afraid to show any sentiment to his canine inmate, and this was not good for the image he had created of being tough and in control. However, it was obvious to those conducting the experiment that he had been affected and did show some emotion to his furry friend. Further experiments revealed that the inmate's emotional metamorphosis transcended mere physical contact with the dogs. In fact, both canines and inmates were connected to bio-energy monitors that showed conclusively that there was some sort of an exchange of energy between canine and human. It was concluded that the canines were somehow able to mentally monitor molecular changes in the atmosphere surrounding the human inmates, enabling the creatures to process this subtle release of energy within seconds. Furthermore, once the canine had discharged the subtle release the inmate affected experienced an incredible release of endorphins - the brain's natural pain killing agents. This probably accounted for the noticeable change of mood each one appeared to exhibit and also why dogs have an extremely calming effect on an anxious mind.

In Russia experiments were conducted into the mental homing device of dogs, and it was found that 9 out of 10 dogs knew exactly when his or her owner was coming home. In fact, in all cases the dog owners had arranged to make their way home at a specified time, and exactly half an hour before they arrived each dog would be at his or her post waiting patiently. These, incidentally, were not cases were the dogs had become accustomed to their owners' routine, as the routine in all cases involved in the experiment had been completely altered and the times randomly chosen. Furthermore, most of the dogs involved in the experiments could even identify the sound of their owner's cars, and when he or she returned home unexpectedly the faithful furry creature was waiting lovingly at the door.

Science has proved beyond a shadow of doubt that animals do possess these abilities, and that they are not peculiar to the canine family alone. Cats too, often exhibit extraordinary abilities, particularly where their owners are concerned and, although dogs appear to be extremely telepathic, experiments have shown that cats are more so.

HEALTH DETECTOR DOGS

Edward Messer, a Tallahassee police officer became concerned when he noticed that the inch-long birthmark on his back had begun changing both in texture and colour. Fearing the worst, he had a biopsy taken from it and was relieved when the results proved negative. However, when the birthmark kept on changing, he insisted that a further biopsy be taken – but this too proved negative. A friend suggested that he should see Duane Pickel, a cancer sniffing dog trainer. After all, he had nothing to lose, and so he went along to be subjected to the canine analysis. Duane Pickel's two dogs homed-in immediately to the lesion on his back, indicating to their owner that the birthmark was most definitely a melanoma. Knowing that his dogs were never wrong with their diagnoses, Duane Pickel advised Edward Messer to have the birthmark removed as soon as possible. The lesion was sent to a pathologist, who made a detailed analysis of it cell by cell. The whole process took four and half days, after which time it was concluded that it was in fact a melanoma. The doctors were forced to admit that they had been wrong in their diagnosis, and that Duane Pickel's dogs had been spot on! Mr Pickel remarked 'the medical community never looked at cancer through anything but a visualisation method. A dog looks at everything through its nose. As a matter of fact, they're the same as a magnetic resonance imaging (MRI) machine – they're both looking for chemical changes.'

Scientific researchers are now trying desperately to determine what it is that dogs recognise as cancer – a protein, an enzyme, an anti-body, so that they can include it in their diagnostic toolbox.

The sensitivity of dogs is also used by Tallahassee dermatologist Armond Cognetta, M.D, a pioneering researcher studying dogs' potential to detect skin cancer. His work completely changed the mind of one sufferer. After numerous tests, doctors assured Natalie Tyler that the blemish on her shoulder was nothing to worry about, even though it continued to grow. Natalie's sister eventually persuaded her to consult Doctor Cognetta who introduced her to two dogs, a Schnauzer named

George and a Golden Labrador called Breeze. These were in fact champion canine sniffers also owned and trained by Duane Pickel. After only one meeting the two dogs were able to sniff and pinpoint the offending lesion on her shoulder. As the two dogs had never been wrong in their 'diagnosis', Doctor Cognetta advised Natalie Tyler to have the mark immediately removed. After 15 years with the mark on her shoulder, it was removed. The dogs had been correct; the mark was a malignant melanoma. Thanks to George and Breeze Natalie's life was saved. Although presently only in its pioneering stages, dog sniffing will be an integral part of diagnostic medicine in the future.

Dogs have also been found to calm the anxieties of Alzheimer sufferers, making them less agitated. Experiments carried out at the School of Veterinary Medicine's Centre for Animal Society, University of California, Davis, concluded that Alzheimer's patients were also less aggressive and anxious when they were accompanied by a dog they were fond of. In fact, Lynette Hart, Ph.D., the Centre's director, said that 'Animals have a normal-ising effect on the behaviour of someone with Alzheimers.' It would appear that this animal therapy is not in any way limited to dogs or cats. On the contrary, all animals whether finned or furred somehow have a remarkable effect upon Alzheimer sufferers. 'Pets are like fur-covered pressure-relief valves that allow us to decompress', remarked one therapist at the Centre.

Although it is fairly common knowledge that cats can see better in the dark than we can, research has shown that the images they perceive are not very clear. Cats' eyes are in fact anatomically similar to ours and according to veterinary textbooks possess two different types of receptor cells – cones and rods, just like humans. According to the experts 'cones' aid resolution and mean that the vision can be clearly focused to enable us to see objects, whilst 'rods' aid our night vision.

Although cat's eyes have more rods than humans, they do possess fewer cones, so whilst they can see better in the dark than humans, their vision is not at all clear!

A dog's hearing is capable of detecting sounds of 35,000 vibrations per second, a cat's hearing 25,000 vibrations per second, and a man's a mere 20,000 vibrations per second. This means that your dog is able to hear you coming down the street and in nearly all cases is able to identify your footsteps and even the sound of your car engine. We often underestimate the powers of our pets and nearly always take their abilities for granted. Although a cat's hearing is not quite as acute as a dog's, it is still capable of detecting sounds that a dog cannot.

Ever since I can remember there was always a dog in my home. In fact, whilst I love and respect all animals, dogs are closer to my heart than any other animal. It was my deep interest in the Animal Kingdom as a whole that led me to collate the information for this book. The scientific facts and observations I have made over the years will hopefully leave no doubt in your mind as to the extraordinary healing powers of animals. If you are one of those people who simply do not like animals at all, for whatever reason, then I am quite certain that you will completely disregard the subject matter of this book as fanciful and far-fetched. All that I can say is that all the facts are there; science is now beginning to change its previous ideas to reach new conclusions about the effect animals have upon our lives. Please do not dismiss the subject matter of this book on one reading alone. Read it again when you have had time to digest the contents.

Pet healing is by no means a new concept, and it is known that the ancient Greeks encouraged the incurably ill to take a horseback ride to raise their spirits. Seventeenth century monasteries in England used cats and dogs to calm the mentally ill, and the residents of the monastic asylums would very often live their lives alongside canine and feline carers. Veterans of both World Wars would often receive pet therapy in hospital to aid their recovery from fatigue, known today as Post-Traumatic Stress Disorder.

Whilst I have always been a dog lover, over the last five years I have become acquainted with two pussycats, an elderly Siamese called 'Suki', and a black and white pussycat called 'Pesi', now sadly both deceased. When I was feeling low and under the weather so to speak, both of these pussycats would gravitate to my lap, I am sure in an effort to reassure and uplift me. It worked each time!

One Alzheimer's patient became so agitated and disturbed that it took Zoe a black Labrador to calm him down. The two became inseparable and there are now even signs the sufferer's periods of agitation are decreasing in frequency. The facts are there that animals most certainly do play an important part in the evolution of our spiritual consciousness, simply by allowing us to be an integral part of their lives.

Science is waking up to the fact that having a pet is most certainly life enhancing, and that when we have a pet we visit the doctor less frequently.

I have mentioned elsewhere in this book that dogs have the exceptional ability to detect molecular changes in the atmosphere, enabling them to give an advance warning of an approaching seizure to sufferers of epilepsy. In fact, epilepsy-alert dogs work in much the same way as cancer sniffing dogs, detecting subtle changes in body odour and fluctuations in a person's electromagnetic atmosphere. The benefits of this early warning detection can very often be lifesaving, particularly when a dog is able to 'sense' a seizure 20 minutes before it actually happens, giving the sufferer sufficient time to prepare themselves.

Alex Lyons belongs to the National Search and Rescue Dog Association. His collie dog Aitken is used to finding people lost on Dartmoor, and has successfully rescued five people within six years. Aitken is now helped by his friend, a Labrador called Ki, the Cornish name for dog. When asked how he thought his dogs were able to do what they do, Alex Lyons said, 'our dogs simply recognise human odours, unlike police tracker dogs who are trained to distinguish smells and are given items of clothing to sniff.'

Humans are somehow biologically programmed to like animals. Although this is not the case with everyone, even those who dislike dogs or cats cannot help being affected by them when they are in their presence. In Canada, St Johns Ambulance have now enlisted the help of dogs in a canine therapy programme to help sufferers of Alzheimers. It has been found that once those suffering from the debilitating disease come into contact with a canine therapist, they become calmer, less aggressive and more coherent. Historically animals have been used to aid humans in their recovery from some sort of illness. After the Second World War, pet therapy was used to aid the recovery of those suffering from combat fatigue, known today as post-traumatic stress disorder. Today science is taking a serious look at the way in which having a pet of some sort affects our health and well-being. Pet therapy is not confined to cats and dogs. On the contrary, there is evidence to suggest that that even birds and fish are extremely therapeutic. Holding a pet rabbit or even a hamster encourages the release of endorphins in the human brain, promoting well-being and relaxing a stressful mind. So, it's a fact then, having a pet of any kind is good for the health!

Research has shown that dogs and cats have some sort of a telepathic relationship with their owners, and sometimes know exactly what their owners are thinking. As I have previously said, that sudden decision to take your dog for a walk, or even to feed your cat, may not have come into your mind of its own accord! Your dog and cat may have sent you the idea. This may well be the reason why he or she is already waiting patiently for you to shift yourself from your chair. What about that then?

When you're not feeling too well, have you noticed that your pussycat seems to be clingier?

After his four year programme researching the behaviour of cats and dogs around their owners, Professor Dawe, an American neurologist working at Budapest University in the early fifties, concluded that having pets around the home affected the movement of chemicals in the human brain, and thus precipitated significant therapeutic changes. Professor Dawe's conclusions came when he brought home a Burmese cat for his four-year-old autistic daughter. The obvious bond between his daughter, Elaine, and her new friend, Miggy, was immediate. In fact, it was quite clear to professor Dawe and his wife that his daughter responded to the Burmese cat in a way she did not respond to them. The family's new pussycat somehow knew that the little girl was 'different' and seemed to treat her in a very special way. This left very little doubt in professor Dawe's mind that there was definitely an exchange of energy between the Burmese cat and his daughter, and that this exchange of energy not only caused a very special bond to form between the two, but also seemed to affect his daughter psychologically speaking.

MORE EVIDENCE

With the support of a team from Warwick University, Chartered Psychologist Dr June McNicholas discovered something quite interesting during her research into the effects of Pet Power. Even long-term depression may be alleviated simply by being around dogs, and that the holistic effects of having a pet can be quite amazing. This brings a whole new meaning to the saying: ' A pat a day keeps the doctor away.'

Dogs particularly have the incredible ability to monitor molecular changes in their owner's personal energy field, and it is this amazing 'homing' device that tells your dog when you are not feeling too well. Using the same device, dogs are able to detect molecular changes in the atmosphere of volcanic areas, and for this reason are used as 'early warning systems', often detecting an approaching volcanic eruption up to 48 hours before it actually occurs. Little wonder then that dogs are trained to 'sniff' out drugs that have been hidden in cargo or the homes of drug dealers! It's true then, dogs are amazing creatures!

Some years ago a small booklet was published by a well known animal food company exploring *Pet Power*. The booklet highlighted the unusual powers our pets have over us, and offered scientific evidence of how the health benefits from having a furry creature around the home. This was not mere conjecture but evidence based on pure scientific facts. The progress of the health of some patients was carefully monitored after regular visits from P.A.T dogs (Pets as Therapy), and the findings of the studies were quite remarkable. In some cases the psychological status of the patients improved by 100 per cent, particularly where those suffering from acute depression or even a terminal illness were concerned. In most of these cases improvement was spontaneous, and in others the process of recovery was gradual, but did continue until the patient was psychologically back to normal.

The Royal College of Veterinary Surgeons now acknowledges the fact that animals do produce some positive changes in both the body and the mind of a person who is elderly or infirm. Although the reassuring warmth of the creature's fur obviously contributes to the whole healing process, research has shown that far more than this takes place upon contact with our pet. Both dogs and cats discharge a hormone that somehow causes the invalid's endorphins to be released. As previously explained these are the body's own painkilling chemicals that also have the effect of creating feelings of euphoria. In other words, as well as creating its own healing force on contact with a sick person, the cat or dog also helps to initiate the self-healing process. Although science is able to monitor the animal's actual discharge of energy, as yet it does not fully understand why this process takes place, and what exactly causes it. Initially the P.A.T dog was thought to simply bring comfort because of it being cute, warm and cuddly, but now opinions have most certainly changed. Much, much more takes place when the canine is in the presence of a sick person.

Nature has designed a special olfactory membrane to enable dogs and humans to smell things. However, in dogs this is considerably larger than in humans, which is probably the reason why dogs have longer noses than we do. This sensitive membrane enables the dog to recognise fragrances floating around on the air, then immediately passes on the information about the smell to be processed by the brain. This is exactly the reason why dogs are being used to smell cancer in the bodies of humans, covered in a previous chapter.

CHAPTER THREE

SPIRITUAL NATURE

Although this book is primarily about the healing powers of animals, in our consideration of the therapeutic value of our pets in the home, it is also important to explore the metaphysical profile of dogs and cats. Some people may find this side of an animal's nature a little far-fetched and difficult to accept. However, in order to comprehend exactly how dogs and cats actually discharge this metaphysical healing force into the atmosphere, and how it is taken up by the human organism, we do need to make a detailed analysis of the spiritual side of our pets.

Chakras are subtle vortices of energy, strategically positioned across the surface of the human subtle anatomy. They are like minute electrical transformers, modifying, controlling and distributing the energy as it comes into the body, maintaining balance and health, emotionally, psychologically, spiritually and physically. This process is exactly the same in the animal as it is in the human, although the anatomical differences of animals allow a more efficient facilitation of energy to take place. In fact, both the animal and human are extremely complex beings and are far more than either appears at a physical level. But as this book is about the healing potential of animals, we will confine ourselves to just that. The physical appearance of animals is in fact replicated on a more subtle level, and is labelled 'Etheric.' Although Etheric substance is invisible to the physical eye, it is nonetheless still matter, albeit of a more subtle nature. And so animals are far more than they appear to us physically, and are not just a body and a soul, but a Spirit possessing a soul. Some Christian fundamentalists will no doubt find it quite offensive to hear the suggestion that animals have souls. I offer no apologies for this statement, for this is my belief. At the same time that animals walk in the physical world, they also have their being in the more sublime area of the supersensual universe. This means that other subtle bodies are required to enable them to function in a multidimensional sense. Although man is a sevenfold being, possessing seven different bodies, the spiritual potential of animals is far greater. Although controlled by a completely different Spiritual evolutionary process, animals do however share two things in common with their human friends – a soul and an *Etheric Body*. The Etheric body has been equated with the wire frame-like structure upon which the sculpture moulds the clay. It in fact replicates the physical form and is responsible for the assimilation of energy coming into it from the sun. The Etheric Body is a network of Etheric wiring, and it is through this extremely complex processing system that our furry friends are able to transmit this powerful healing force directly into the surrounding atmosphere. I am sure that only a minority of the animal Kingdom consciously transmit this healing force directly to its human carer, but I am in no doubt that all animals unconsciously create that healing balm that is so important for the maintenance of mans' emotional and psychological equilibrium. In fact, both cats and dogs are like dynamos, continually creating and discharging the healing energy, which is thus quickly taken up by the human nervous system. This healing process takes place regardless of whether or not one is an animal lover. However, it is somehow far more effective once our furry friend has won his or her way into our heart. Even though science would no doubt dismiss this concept as 'poppycock' and New Age nonsense, the fact is, many people do believe that animals are driven by the same spirit that drives us humans; and that spirit can NEVER die! We should never underestimate that all-important wag of the tail, which is the healing smile of a loving friend. I am always reminded of that saying: '*A house without a pet is just a house.*'

CHAPTER FOUR

LET'S NOT FORGET CATS!

Although it was previously thought that cats could seek out their owners several hundreds of miles away, purely by instinct, apparently this is not quite the case. Researchers have discovered that cats have a complex navigational system in their brains that allows them to calculate their route home simply by gauging the position of the sun or moon in the heavens. That's an amazing feat when you think about it. Of course, some instinct is involved for them to 'know' exactly where their owner is residing.

Traditionally cats have always been creatures of mystery and intrigue, which is probably why witches of bygone days seemed to nearly always be accompanied by their black 'Familiars', a loyal cat that somehow added that extra mystique. In ancient Egypt cats were revered as sacred and mystical creatures and would grace the homes of the wealthy as well as the palaces of royalty. The Egyptians made a powerful ointment with cat's excrement combined with special herbs. This allegedly had an incredible healing effect when applied to infected wounds and other bodily conditions. This sounds repulsive and is certainly not recommended. However, the cat played such an integral part in every day ancient Egyptian life, that they would be buried alive with their dead owners, primarily to ensure their safe delivery into the afterlife.

In ancient Siam cats were also regarded as holy creatures. The Siamese cat was a ferocious creature trained primarily to protect the king or queen. However, as well as protectors of the throne, Siamese cats were also hunters and were encouraged to be fierce and aggressive. I am quite sure though that today their ferociousness has been bread out of them. For six years I was fortunate to share my life with a Siamese pussycat called Suki, a very gentle and extremely wise creature that, I am sure, had been here many, many times before. Suki always knew when I was feeling unwell or simply under the weather. Although she never really liked to be cuddled or even held in anyway whatsoever, when I was feeling unwell she would always make a beeline for my lap. Suki was extremely persistent and would remain close to me until she knew I was feeling better, and she was always right.

Apart from this though cats have always been regarded as special and were thought to possess 'something' in their fur that could ease aching limbs and calm taut nerves. Some of you may remember your grandmother cuddling her cat in front of the fire on a cold winter's day, and saying 'She eases my aching joints!' Too many elderly people made that statement for it not to be true. Besides, your grannies were not the only ones who derived some benefit from cats. The Elizabethan apothecaries frequently recommended 'cat therapy' in one form or another. For shingles and other maladies of the nervous system, they prescribed an infusion of herbs, vinegar and honey in a horrid concoction blended with the blood from a cat's ear. To ease the pains of arthritis and gout cat fur would be draped across the bed in the winter months. In fact, the Elizabethans swore by it, and even though one needed to be quite wealthy, it was quite fashionable to have a cat fur bedspread draped across the four-poster bed.

Although I have always been a dog person, gradually over the years I have grown very fond of cats. In fact, today my wife and I are privileged to have two pussycats, Poppy and her sister Elly, a long haired tortoise-shell. Both of these are extremely loving and seem to know when either my wife or myself is not feeling too well. In fact, I have over the years come to the conclusion that all cats are feline doctors and possess a natural need to care for humans. Like dogs they too have an in-built instinct that enables them to monitor molecular changes in a person's energy field. Although cats have not been studied as much as dogs for their healing abilities, any cat lover will vouch for the therapeutic value of having a cat as a pet.

THE LIFE FORCE

In esoteric parlance *Prana* is a universal energy – the presence of which sustains life. Prana is believed to be drawn into the physical body via breathing, and the more prana that enters and remains in the body, the higher the quality of life. A reduction in the body's levels of prana results in the lowering of their vitality and a marked deterioration of the health. It is known that some people have great stores of prana in their bodies, and just being in their presence is uplifting and invigorating. Although dogs possess great stores of this energy in their bodies, cats are believed to have so much of it that they exude pranic energy in incredible streams, particularly through their tails. People who do not like cats, tend to have very poor reserves of prana in their nervous systems. As a result of this a cat will always gravitate towards those who do not like them, perhaps in an asserted effort to infuse the individual with something it has in abundance. The cat will first of all encircle the person's legs, usually with a 'figure eight' motion, purring and arching its back with its tail held high in an 'S' shape. Should the person be brave enough to sit down then the cat will make an attempt to sit on his or her lap, purring and occasionally shifting its furry position. If this fails to work, at least the person will go away feeling a little more vitalised and uplifted. Even though they may be totally oblivious to the reason they feel like this, at least the pussycat will have done its job!

Don't take my word for it, try this little experiment:

- *Sitting next to your cat, place your fingertips gently on your solar plexus, (the area just below your ribcage.)*
- *With your eyes closed, breathe rhythmically until the rhythm is fully established, then imagine that with each inhalation streams of intense white light are being drawn through your nostrils, into*

your lungs, and then into your solar plexus, where it passes into your fingertips.

- Hold your breath whilst carrying the white light in your fingertips to your pussycat, on the part of its back just by its tail, without touching its fur.

- Still holding your breath, point your outstretched fingers to your cat, and as you breathe out, move your fingers (as though playing the piano) and your hands from tail to head, imagining streams of white light discharging from your fingertips, infusing your cat with vitality.

- If your pussycat has still not moved, repeat the whole process again until it does.

- Your cat should suddenly sit up quickly (as though it's had a shock) arching its back, and extending its tail into an 'S' shape as it moves quickly away from you.

- During the process, remember not to actually touch your cat with your hands, as it is then more evidential when it moves.

The whole process suddenly increases your cat's vitality, causing a sudden surge of energy through its body, a similar experience to an electric shock or a splash of icy cold water. The experiment is quite harmless to your pussycat, and produces this effect because you are infusing it with the vitality it really does not need. However, when your cat is elderly or unwell, it would benefit from this extremely powerful and therapeutic treatment, which would be like a 'tonic' to it, aiding its recovery.

CHAPTER FIVE

FURRY TAILS

I am quite sure that only a dog lover will appreciate what I mean when I say there's nothing like a cold nose on the face when one is feeling depressed or a little under the weather. Although our canine friend can express his or her love in many different ways, that all-important wag and the cold wet nose says it all. In fact, there are innumerable stories of how humans have been helped from their depression by his or her loving canine friend. The story of John Baxter's life-long fight with depression is one that was related to me by John himself. He had been suffering with depression since he was eighteen years old, and although he had a good job and a loving family, these were not sufficient to keep the overwhelming dark clouds of depression at bay. It would often happen quite suddenly and for no one apparent reason. One minute he could be on top of the world and the next down in the pits of despair. John's illness was medically defined as indigenous depression and as he had suffered with it for many years, the clinical prognosis was quite bleak.

It really all changed for John when he and his wife Mandy decided to buy their seven-year-old son Michael an Old English Sheep dog. Blink, the new family member settled in quickly to the Baxter residence and immediately brought the family routine into chaos. The boisterous furry family member demanded everyone's total attention, and although the dog was supposed to be young Michael's pet, Blink, as they had called him, always seemed to gravitate to John, particularly when he was in one of his deep depressions. Gradually over the next six months Blink became John's constant companion. His bouts of depression lessened and, only 9 months after Blink had joined the family,

John appeared to everyone to be a new man. Today three years on John Baxter's depression is a thing of the past. 'I can't really remember what it's like to be depressed anymore!' remarked John when I spoke to him. 'I don't have the time these days to be depressed.' Those who know John Baxter will say that he has changed completely. His psychiatrist too is amazed with the metamorphosis in his personality and the profound change in his outlook on life.

MOJI TO THE RESCUE

Sarah Reed suffered for many years with depression and had even attempted suicide on two occasions. Her mental state deteriorated after the death of her mother, and now at the age of fifty-two her future looked quite bleak. Sarah also suffered with a chronic anxiety neurosis and was terrified to leave the safety of her home. Agoraphobia brought on by her long-term depression was in fact diagnosed. Her doctor was baffled. He had known Sarah for over twenty years and had noticed the gradual and yet very dramatic change in her psychological status. Although medication kept Sarah fairly stable, each day was a nightmare and she just felt that there was nothing at all to live for. Life though suddenly changed when Ron her husband read an article about pet therapy in a woman's magazine. 'Dogs can make you well!' the article read. 'Living with animals is good for the health!' Although they had never had a pet of any description Ron was willing to try anything to make his wife well again. Prior to her illness she had always been fun to be with and was always smiling. He would do anything to see that again and so went to the local Animal Rescue Centre to get a dog. As a child Ron had been brought up with a Golden Labrador and so he knew only too well how gentle and friendly they could be. And so when he saw Moji the 5-year-old Golden Labrador sitting quietly in his kennel, Ron knew right away that this was the one.

Moji took to the family immediately, and the canine's effect upon Sarah was instantaneous. It demanded all her attention and would simply not leave her alone. This made Ron smile to himself, as he knew that most of Sarah's depression appeared to happen when she was sitting there thinking. Moji would not allow Sarah to sit idly and constantly prodded her with his nose, seemingly in an effort to initiate a game. It seemed now that Sarah was laughing all the time and was never seen to be depressed. Within six months, to everyone's surprise Sarah was off her medication and appeared to be back to her old happy self. Ron was certain that his wife's recovery was due to Moji's presence in the home. That was two years ago now and Sarah has not looked back. She goes for long walks with Moji in the nearby park and has no fear whatsoever of open spaces. For Sarah depression is now a thing of the past, thanks to Moji.

KITTEN ON THE KEYS

Lizzy Beck was only 56 years old when she suffered her first stroke. She was an accomplished pianist and had taught music for over 25 years in a prestigious London College. Lizzy's friends had said that it was her music that helped her to recover so quickly. However, just when she was getting herself back to normal she had a second stroke. This one though affected her speech and impaired her mobility greatly. Because Lizzy's hands had been affected by the second stroke she could not carry on teaching the piano. This made her even more withdrawn and depressed. Her husband, Peter tried everything he could to encourage his wife to make the effort. But Lizzy had given up on everything and just sat in the chair all day staring out at the garden.

The family already had a black Labrador and an elderly pussycat called 'Bong'. A friend showed Peter an article in a magazine about a cat that had aided its owner's recovery from a serious stroke. Peter had noticed that since Lizzy's illness Bong had been very clingy and took every opportunity to gravity to his wife's lap. Although Bong's demonstration of affection never failed to encourage a response from Lizzy, her condition showed no signs of improvement. However, everything began to change when a family friend brought Lizzy a black kitten. The boisterous eight-week-old pussycat had been made an orphan when her mother died giving birth. Lizzy's eyes widened when the kitten was placed on her lap. She couldn't avoid steadying the little cat with her hand to prevent it from falling from her knee. It was obvious that Lizzy's senses had been dramatically activated by the clawing pussycat's presence. Within only half an hour Lizzy was making an effort to talk, if only to ask her friend to take the kitten from her.

Things really started to change for Lizzy when, a few days later the mischievous kitten found its way onto the keys of the piano. She watched with delight as the little cat marched deliberately over the piano keys, as though picking out the notes she liked the best. Lizzy could not resist the temptation to join in the fun and sat by the piano with her finger on the keys. Peter stood in the doorway watching his wife with amazement as she made every effort to play the piano along with the kitten. He couldn't believe what he was seeing. The tiny creature seemed to know exactly what it was doing, and even stopped to watch Lizzy's fingers clumsily pushing down the notes one at a time.

The weeks that followed saw a vast improvement in Lizzy's condition, and within 12 months she was back to near normal. That was three years ago and today Lizzy Beck has returned to the job that she loves so much, teaching music. The little pussycat has established itself well and truly in the home along with the other two furry creatures.

JANGLES RETURNS

Because of George Melling's work both he and his family were moving home and were going to live over three hundred miles away. On the day that they were due to move Jangles, the family's elderly black cat went missing. He had been with the Melling family since he was six weeks old and had become one of the family. They were understandably distraught, particularly George Melling's 12 year old son Michael, with whom Jangles had a special relationship. The family searched the entire district for their cat Jangles, and looked in all the likely places, alas to no avail. Jangles had disappeared completely. George Melling was certain that their elderly pussycat would eventually turn up, and so a close friend and neighbour promised to look out for him.

Three weeks went by and the Melling family had settled into their new home and George into his new job. Twelve-year-old Michael had started at a new boarding school that meant that he was away most of the term. But Jangles had still not returned.

One November afternoon Michael was playing football on the school playing field when he saw a black cat running across the field towards him. He couldn't believe that it was Jangles the family cat. Although a little worse for the three hundred plus miles journey, Jangles was in good condition and was returned safely to his new home. Although all the family loved Jangles, he was in fact regarded as Michael's pet, with whom he obviously had a special affinity. The story of Jangles is quite amazing when you come to think of it. However, the fact that Michael's new boarding school had only been decided two weeks before the Mellings' house move makes the whole scenario even more incredible. This story though is not unusual, and there have been numerous accounts of cats travelling hundreds of miles to be with their owner. It is really only in the last ten years that interest has turned towards the unusual abilities of animals and the effect that they have over their owners. In fact today there is a whole new concept of animal psychology, and it is now realised that animals play a vitally important part in the evolution of mans' emotional and psychological well being.

EARLY WARNING BARK

Epilepsy had been diagnosed when Katy Waring was just fourteen years old. Although now at seventeen her condition was under control, because of the severity of her fits it was imperative that her medication should be administered as early as possible. All the years of fitting nearly every day had taken its toll on Katy's life and, although her general health was quite good she suffered from severe bouts of weakness and lethargy.

Katy had always loved dogs and had a two-year-old Jack Russell called Jack as her constant companion. The two were inseparable, and whenever possible she would take Jack for long walks on the nearby common. One day whilst walking home Jack began barking excitedly and pushing Katy with his nose. She hadn't a clue what was wrong with him, and tried everything without success to make him quiet. Suddenly Jack ran off in the direction of home. Katy called after him but the little dog kept on running. Upon seeing Jack at the front door alone, Katy's mother was quite concerned. The little dog barked excitedly at her as though he wanted her to follow him. Katy's mother was certain that her daughter was in some kind of difficulty and so followed Jack as he took off down the street. As she reached the end of the street she noticed one of her neighbours stooping over her daughter who was lying on the floor fitting. Katy's mother knew exactly what to do, and within minutes Katy had regained consciousness. Although she was disorientated for a few minutes, she was all right and hadn't hurt herself when she collapsed.

Both Katy and her mother soon realised that their little dog had somehow known about Katy's fit in advance. They later found out that dogs were being trained to accompany acute Epilepsy sufferers and to detect the onset of an attack up to 24 hours before it actually happens. Jack had not been trained and yet he did this instinctively. Katy's condition improved even more over the next twelve months as a result of little Jack's acute warning device. Because of a canine's sensing ability they are able to detect molecular changes in the atmosphere around the Epilepsy sufferer. As a result of this Jack transformed Katy's life and gave her confidence and support. It was Katy's little dog's sensitivity that encouraged Katy and transformed her life.

TIGER'S HEALING PAWS

Margaret Dawson has had Tiger the 10-year-old tabby since she was a kitten. Although the cuddly pussycat had always been extremely affectionate, it was really only in the last 2 years that Tiger had developed the unusual practice of sleeping across her mistress's shoulders when she was relaxing in the chair. Margaret noticed that her pussycat only did this when her back was playing up, usually in the cold winter months. However, Margaret had to admit that Tiger's sleeping position had an incredible effect upon the pain in her back, and within minutes after she had climbed on to her mistress's shoulders, the pain would be eased.

Margaret's husband was very sceptical and doubted very much that it was Tiger who was responsible for the pain's easement. 'The pain's in your back!' he scoffed. 'Not in your neck.'

It was only after a scan and extensive investigations that the hospital consultant concluded that a trapped nerve at the base of her skull was in fact responsible for Margaret's back pain. 'Scoff now,' laughed Margaret to her husband. 'Tiger knew all the time.' And Margaret's husband had to admit that it looked as though she was right and he was most definitely wrong.

THE PAW OF ENCOURAGEMENT

Tom Betterman's family thought that he was surely going to die when he had his second and more severe stroke. He could not speak now and was completely unable to move his left arm at all. More than this though Tom was extremely depressed and refused to eat. A family friend knew someone who had a PAT dog called

Jamie and it was she who suggested that the little Scottie dog should be introduced to Tom. Although initially Tom's family declined the offer on the grounds that they believed that Tom needed specialised medical help and not a canine visitor, as they had nothing to lose, they eventually agreed.

Upon meeting Tom, Jamie immediately went to work. The canine sat at Tom's feet, occasionally pushing him with his nose in an effort to initiate a stroke. Although Tom was unable to move his left hand at all, he did at least make an effort to reach out to Jamie with his right hand. After a few attempts Tom gave up, a look of frustration showing across his pale face. This somehow made Jamie more determined and he proffered a paw to Tom causing a smile to show slightly across his thin lips.

Jamie came every day to see Tom and within four weeks a slight improvement could be seen in the movement of his left arm.

It took no more than six months and Tom was able to walk unaided and could even speak again. That was two years ago and Tom Betterman is now leading a near normal life, thanks to Jamie's encouragement and, an abundance of love and healing.

JENNY'S GONE HOME

The Anson family all agreed that the family's new Alsatian dog should be called 'Jenny', a suitable name for an extremely friendly creature with an agreeable and very loving nature. Although Jenny had been bought as a pet for the children of the house, Sydney Anson was quite surprised when the family's new addition seemed to attach herself to him, and followed him everywhere. In fact, the two became inseparable and went every-where together. When Sydney Anson retired for the night, usually after midnight, Jenny would finish the last of her dinner, and then patiently await her loving master's whistle, telling her that it was time for her to join him upstairs. Although Jenny was never allowed on the bed, she did sleep on a large cushion next to the dressing table, and even had her own warm duvet. The whole family had now accepted the fact that Jenny was their father's dog, and they had all become accustomed to the familiar whistle just after midnight.

The years went by and Sydney Anson was diagnosed with terminal cancer. Being the loving family man he was, he insisted that he should spend his last weeks at home with his family. He would frequently be found sitting on the stairs struggling for breath, his faithful companion sitting by his side. Although everyone was deeply saddened when Sydney finally lost his battle against his illness, Jenny found it very difficult to function without her loving master. She wouldn't eat and quickly went into a deep depression. The vet had warned the family that they should not expect Jenny to live any longer than a few days. Sydney's daughter, Jane nursed Jenny in front of the fire, and on the evening when she drew in her last breath, Jane heard the unmistakable sound of her father whistling from upstairs. Jane's mother also heard it, and her brother who was usually a heavy sleeper, quickly came down stairs to see if everyone else had heard it! At least now the grieving family were comforted to know that their father was all right, and that he and Jenny were now together. 'Jenny has gone home, mum!' smiled Jane to her mother. 'She's with dad again!'

BORIS

Boris was the most unlikely name for a Jack Russel, but that was the name Dorothy and Jim Taylor chose for the little stray who wandered into their home one cold and blustery afternoon. He wasn't a young dog and had obviously lived somewhere. However, from the condition of his coat, Jim had concluded that he had been living on the streets for some time.

After the usual enquiries around the neighbourhood, the desk sergeant at the local police station made a note of their address and told the Taylors to take the little dog home with them. They were delighted, and Boris settled in to his new home very quickly, and within a few days the friendly dog had completely familiarised himself with his new surroundings. The little dog obviously liked his new home and showed no signs at all of fretting. In no time at all Boris became one of the Taylor family and even had his own little armchair at the side of the fireplace.

A whole year had gone by and Jim and Boris had just returned from the park, an exercise that had almost become a daily ritual, and something, which Doris said, kept Jim healthy.

It was November and by 4pm a thick blanket of fog had suddenly descended. Doris peered through the curtains and remarked that she could not even see the garden gate. Jim suddenly remembered that the car was still parked on the road, and rose tiredly from the chair. 'I'll put it in the garage before it gets any later', he said making his way through the door. But as soon as Boris saw his master leave the room, he jumped from his chair and quickly followed him.

Unaware that Boris was behind him Jim reluctantly pulled back the front door to face the icy fog with a shiver. Before he had a chance to do anything Boris had run passed him. Jim called him in a stern, authoritative voice, but the little dog ignored his master and ran off into the thick fog before finally disappearing through a hole in the privet.

Jim and Doris did not think for one moment that Boris would not return when they called him, but to their great sadness their little dog had gone.

The weeks passed by and there was still no sign of the Taylor's little Jack Russell. He was greatly missed, especially by Jim who looked upon little Boris as his friend.

Two months had passed by and Jim and Doris had returned from town after a very tiring shopping trip. Jim looked particularly exhausted and so Doris suggested that he go to bed for an hour whilst she prepared the evening the meal. Jim had no sooner left the room when Doris heard a loud noise. She rushed to the hallway to see Jim lying on the floor at the foot of the stairs. He had obviously suffered a heart attack and so she phoned immediately for an ambulance. Happily, it was only a minor attack brought on, the doctor told her, by extreme fatigue. The prognosis was positive; a lot of rest and some tender, loving care was all that was required to help Jim back on the road to recovery.

The weeks passed by and Jim's recovery was extremely slow. He seemed quite depressed and was not eating. His general condition was surprisingly good, but Jim had seemingly lost all interest in life. Doris knew that he was missing his companion little Boris. She suggested getting another dog but Jim would not hear of it.

It was Thursday night and Doris was making a cup of tea for her husband when she heard a scratching sound at the kitchen door. She went to investigate and could not believe what greeted her when she pulled back the door. Little Boris was sitting patiently on the step. He stood there wagging his tail for a few moments then bolted past Doris to immediately make his way upstairs to where Jim was lying in bed. The little dog jumped onto the bed and began excitedly licking his master's face. Jim couldn't believe that his little friend had come home, almost as though he had known Jim was unwell. Whatever the reason for Boris's return, it hastened Jim's recovery, and within a week the two were taking their daily walks again.

THE FOURLEGGED ANGEL

Joan Pierce had had her Siamese pussycat, Donut, since she was a kitten. She was now sixteen and beginning to show her age. Joan was dreading the day when she would lose her and wondered what she would do without her constant companion.

It was an extremely warm June afternoon and Joan had opened the patio doors leading onto the garden at the rear of the house. She poured herself a cold drink and went into the garden to relax on the garden chair for a few moments. She was about to sip her well-deserved drink, when she noticed a ginger Tomcat staring at her from a bench at the far end of the garden. She had never seen this cat before and wondered who it belonged to. Joan sat for a few minutes talking to the cat, and when she had finished her drink she went inside to get some of Donut's food for it. At first it was a little weary, but realising Joan meant him no harm, he devoured it within seconds.

The Ginger Tom visited Joan's garden every day. It appeared early morning and remained on the bench at the far end of the garden until nightfall. The ginger Tom never missed a day, and regardless of how bad the weather was, he would always appear in the garden. Joan made every attempt to coax the cat into her home, but it refused to move from the bench at the far end of the garden. This continued for a further two weeks, until one morning Joan opened her patio doors to be greeted by the ginger Tom waiting to come in. This time the ginger cat couldn't wait to get inside the house. He headed straight for Donut's dish and devoured every bit of her Tuna chunks. He then made his way into the living room and settled on the settee and fell fast asleep. It looked like Donut had a new friend and Joan now had an extra mouth to feed.

Although Donut was normally antisocial and very possessive where Joan was concerned, the Siamese befriended the ginger Tomcat very quickly and they became inseparable. In no time at all the ginger cat settled into his new home and was given the appropriate name of Jinjy, which suited him perfectly.

Two months passed by, and to Joan's great sadness, Donut suddenly fell into a decline and passed away. Joan was mortified and felt as though she had lost one of her family. However, she now realised why Jinjy had suddenly appeared in the garden, seemingly from nowhere. Although deeply saddened by the death of her Siamese friend Donut, she was certain that Jinjy had been sent from heaven to take her pussycat's place. Although Jinjy was not Donut, she was so thankful that he had chosen her garden, and chosen it she was certain he had for a special reason. He was her four legged angel, and an angel who came in her time of great sadness.

CHAPTER SIX

ANIMAL MAGIC

A whole new concept of *Animal Magic* is opening up to us today, and as we move further into the millennium Golden Age, more and more people are developing the realization that animals are extremely special and vitally important to the spiritual and emotional evolution of mankind.

Animals too appear to be developing an awareness of humans, to the extent that many wild species are becoming quite tame, and are appearing to show very little fear of us. Next time you walk down the High Street just take a look at the way pigeons and sparrows walk about your feet, completely unperturbed by your presence. When you are sitting quietly in your garden see how close Robins and Blackbirds come to you, and how squirrels and even rabbits seem almost oblivious to your presence.

Man's collective awareness is having a profound effect on the wild animals and on nature. Although science informs us that the planet is in a sorry state due to our ignorance and abuse of it, there is an extremely significant spiritual epoch beginning to dawn across the face of mankind; in fact, the Golden Age of Spirit.

The birds of the air, the fish of the oceans and the creatures of the fields and meadows are crying out with a desperate need to be allowed to share this life on which man believes he has the sole monopoly, and so therefore has exploited selfishly to the full.

All creatures, whether of the air, the land or the sea possess healing powers peculiar to their own species. Although most of these creatures will never have any contact with human life, their energies are continually discharged into the environment, precipitating a vibratory healing motion in the earth's surrounding atmosphere. Animals are the ambassadors of a much higher force than we will ever realize.

One of the cheekiest, most intelligent, and strongest healing birds is the blackbird, whose closeness to us humans has increased over the last 15 years or so. When the bird is in full song its aura becomes a beautiful display of pink, blue and yellow. Perched on the apex of a tall conifer tree, singing its heart out, the Blackbird is aglow with healing rays that can be seen psychically as bright sparks dancing in the air. Not only are these birds a delight to watch, but either listening to them singing or simply watching them play in the garden, creates a great deal of healing, which can be extremely effective when one is feeling under the weather. Apart from the metaphysical effects of birdsong, the psychological ways in which birds affect us must also be considered. There's nothing more relaxing than walking round the garden listening to a blackbird go through its repertoire of varying songs. I'm sure you will agree with me, we all feel so much the better for having heard it? Another playful bird, whose healing skills must not be underestimated, is the Robin. These cheeky and very playful little birds always seem to appear when you are feeling a little depressed or just under the weather. Their melodic tones have an amazing effect upon the human mind.

Although you may not see many chimpanzees roaming the streets of Britain, these creatures, which are so much like us humans, are veritable powerhouses of energy. The healing force is transmuted in their bodies in much the same way as in the human organism. In fact, the chimpanzee's subtle energies are organized in exactly the same way as man's, but with slight differences to the individual areas of the subtle anatomy. This indicates that the chimpanzee's consciousness has not quite developed to the level of its human brother, and it still uses faculties that man has long since forgotten about.

I have previously mentioned that research has shown that children brought up with a dog or a cat, are more evenly tempered and much calmer in later life than those brought up in a home without animals. Animals do contribute far more to a house than just a warm, furry presence. In fact, once a dog or a cat establishes itself in the home, family life is never, ever the same again. Anyone who has had a close, loving relationship with either a cat or a dog will no doubt agree that our pets do weave a magical spell upon us, and are forever somewhere in our minds throughout the day. I think it's safe to say that while you are in work your dog or cat comes into your thoughts more than once throughout the day, if only to wonder if he or she is alright. Once that furry relationship has been well and truly established, you can rest assured that they are always in your heart, and never far from your thoughts. My mother would never leave Lucky, her Border Collie alone in the house, at least without the radio or television on to keep him company. I'll bet that 97 out of a 100 people reading this book are exactly the same as my mother, and always make certain that their dog or cat has something to keep it company whilst they are out. Research in both Russia and America has shown that the way our pets affect our emotions is in fact extremely good for our health. Not only do our pets encourage us back to health when we have been ill, but they can also extend our lives by years. Dogs and cats help to lower blood pressure, and can relieve stress and ease pain, particularly in the back. Our pets are somehow able to encourage the release of endorphins (the body's natural pain killers) in the brain, making us feel good, relaxed and pain free. Dogs and cats do have healing paws, and because of their natural abilities to monitor molecular changes around their owners, they somehow 'know' when we are depressed or not well.

CHAPTER SEVEN

ANIMAL SOUL SYSTEM

There are those who would completely dismiss the concept of animals having souls. In fact, many of the early Christian scholars would be repulsed at the very idea of animals living on when they die. St Francis of Assisi was an exception, which is why he is accepted as the patron Saint of animals. His love of animals extended far beyond the confines of earthly love, and it is believed that St Francis could communicate with animals and knew exactly what they were thinking and saying.

Although the evidence of animal survival is a lot less than that which substantiates the survival of the human soul, there are innumerable stories of the way in which animals have helped their owners from beyond the grave. We'll take a look at these later. Now, though, I would like to explore the way in which animals are spiritually connected to their owners and the way they influence us in our everyday lives. My father used to say that 'people who don't like animals have no souls.' I don't think this is strictly true, but I did get the gist of what he was saying. Those who have a deep dislike of animals do lack something spiritually. Some cultures believe that *'Animals are the Unwinged Angels who visit us from afar; they show us how to love and to know exactly who we are.'*

From time immemorial animals have fascinated us, and many famous writers have featured animals in their books. One of these was Beatrix Potter who wrote about nothing else but animals. In fact, she made them almost human, with the ability to speak. There is very little doubt that a world without animals would be a very bleak and extremely miserable place. It has been said that 'Humans need to be in the company of animals to keep them sane and healthy.'

Dogs have always been thought of as man's best friend, which is why they have been shown in innumerable stories as having almost human-like intelligence. Rin-Tin-Tin, the Alsatian dog of the Wild West, always came to the rescue when someone was in dire straits. Lassie too was always there when help was needed. A similar canine figure was Black Bob, the Collie dog who always appeared when its owner was in trouble. Greyfriar's Bobby was the true and very sad story of a faithful terrier that remained by his owner's grave until he himself died. Dogs particularly have always appeared in films as heroes, loving and protecting their human friends. The loving and spiritual bond between man and his dog has always been so strong and apparent, that there must be more to such a relationship than a comforting furry presence. Some dog owners share an almost telepathic relationship with their dogs, and both dog and owner seem to know exactly what the other is thinking. It has been suggested that dogs are able to transmit their desires to their owners, and so when the lead is retrieved from the cupboard, and the call 'Walkies' is given, we know exactly why the loveable dog is already waiting eagerly at the front door. It's easy; your dog sent you the thoughts 'I'm ready to go for my walk now.' Those who have either a cat or a dog as a pet are usually very aware that their lives are controlled by them. In fact, our lives totally revolve around our pets, and although we think that they rely on us, believe me it is totally the other way round, we most certainly rely on them. Once our lives have been touched by a dog or cat, we never think in quite the same way ever again. We even evolve a new and very silly way of talking. 'Who is mummy's little girl? Walkies. Who's a pretty little girl then? Din-dins' And when we feed our little mites, it is very often 'Yummy, yummy, who's a lucky boy?' In an asserted effort to encourage them to eat all their food and clean their dishes. The crazy thing about the way we talk to our pets is that they really do understand it.

We often wrongly assume that we choose our pets, but when we really stop to think about it we can see that it is they who choose us. There is very little doubt in my mind that there is some sort of conspiracy in the animal kingdom, and that they are closer to god than we could ever hope to be. Animals are unaffected by any religious philosophical structure, and with all animals what you see is exactly what you get. Our love is always reciprocated, and even when we are stressed and have no time to show them love, they will still proffer a paw in an attempt to win our affections.

How can we not be affected by those furry creatures with whom we share this planet?

Even though the animal soul system is completely different to that to which we humans are spiritually connected, both dogs and cats can find a soul mate in a human owner. Although not all dogs are gentle, they are all connected one to the other by some intricately woven invisible spiritual network, that affects the human psyche in an extremely subtle and yet very powerful way. You can occasionally see from the look in the eyes of some dogs and cats that they have been here before and that they will not be coming again. I have been fortunate to have two dogs in whose eyes this was quite apparent. Harry was an Old English sheepdog, and was the runt of the litter, or so I was told. He was almost human and his eyes were kind and warm. He was the most playful and gentle dog I have ever known, and it was obvious that this was his last visit to this planet and that he would not be coming again. To someone who doesn't like animals this will sound absurd. But Harry was a spiritual dog who knew that he was on this planet to love and be loved. Unfortunately he had been a sickly dog from the very day he was born, and only lived until he was nine years old. Lucky, too, was kind and gentle, but possessed a completely different temperament to Harry. He was a more considerate little creature with a huge heart. He was a black Border Collie who had been abandoned as a young dog.

My mother took him in and he showed his gratitude right up until the day he died at the age of 14, exactly one month after my mother herself passed away. Lucky was a very much loved dog, and although he was very different to Harry, my Old English sheepdog, I have no doubt whatsoever that Lucky and Harry were the same dog. Reincarnation is not confined to the human soul, animals too often return in response to the call of 'Love.'

Pets most certainly leave a lasting impression on our lives, and sometimes losing them is like losing a member of the family. Losing your pet has an overwhelming effect upon the home. The noticeable absence of that furry presence lying in front of the fire is quite devastating to our emotions. In fact, it produces an awful, deep silence that throbs inside our hearts. The death of a pet affects the human emotions, almost as if an invisible sword had pierced the heart, and we always solemnly swear that no other animal will take its place.

CHAPTER EIGHT

A SMALL PRICE TO PAY

Cat fur all over the bed, walking on broken dog biscuits, or the unavoidable dog or cat fur all over that new black suit, are most certainly prerequisites for having a furry presence in the home. 'A small price to pay!' my mother always said grinning, as I danced angrily round the room, frantically trying in vain to remove my dog's hairs from my black suit. To be quite honest, though, it is a very small price to pay for the love and immense enjoyment our pets give us. It's freezing cold outside with torrential rain and you are sitting comfortably in front of the warm fire watching television. Your attention is caught by your dog, wagging its tail excitedly by the door, its eyes wide willing you to take it on the nightly obligatory walk. What do you do?

A Ignore it completely and let it think you are watching your favourite programme?
B Pretend to be snoozing and hope it will lose interest?
C Be firm and shout angrily at it to go and lie down.

Let's first of all look at A:) Well, to begin with your dog knows very well that you are not watching your favourite programme. Even if you were, so what? It's time for walkies and that's the end of that! (B) Your loyal dog knows exactly when you are asleep, and you know it. Even if you were it's time to do your duty. You've got an obligation, and if your dog could speak it would tell you that you will appreciate your snooze even more after a brisk walk in the pouring cold rain. (C) You can be firm and shout at your dog if you want, but it will only make you feel guilty and very sorry later on. So, everyone knows that nightly walk is inevitable.

It is truly a small price to pay when you see muddy paws all over your clean kitchen floor, or when your pussycat decides to walk on that freshly painted window ledge. Considering the love they give to us, it is a small price to pay when your dog returns from the garden and decides to wipe its dirty bottom across the surface of your new carpet, or when your elderly pussycat slobbers all down the front of your new dress. You either love animals or you don't. I can never understand people who eagerly announce, 'I can't stand dogs and cats,' making us animal lovers feel quite guilty when our boisterous mongrel rushes excitedly into the room, expecting our visitor to be just as keen to meet them. However, it doesn't take our pets very long to sense those who do not like them. Animals do have a radar system that enables them to detect molecular changes in the atmosphere. Unlike dogs cats know immediately, but instead of avoiding those who dislike them they gravitate towards them, mostly in an asserted effort to win their favour. The cat will make sure that their scent is on the person's clothes, and will weave its way in and out of the person's legs, daring them to proffer a hand of approval. The person who dislikes cats is always the first in a room to be targeted. When a person who dislikes cats sits down, the offending feline will always gravitate to his or her knee in a bold attempt to convert them to the universal club of cat lovers. Having an allergic reaction to cats is one thing, but despising them is another and a complete abomination.

Although now somewhat of a cliché, 'A pet is for life and not just for Christmas'. A pet lover will know only too well that it is not difficult to love our pet. Although we nearly always treat our pets like children, in a lot of cases a dog or cat will treat its owner as a child. Anyone who has a pet as a fashion accessory for the home, and for no other reason, will very often find it difficult to understand what their dog or cat is saying to them. Pet lovers do develop a natural telepathic relationship with their pets and generally know instinctively what their furry friend is saying to them. Dogs and cats may not speak with words, but the dialogue they use is most definitely universal and one that transcends the confines of speech. It is believed that before our prehistoric forebears developed even the most rudimentary form of speech, they most probably communicated their thoughts and feeling telepathically. One notable writer once said that man only developed speech so that he could tell lies. Whether or not the latter statement is true, one thing is certain our pets do make an effort to communicate with us, so why shouldn't we make the effort to understand them. This is probably the biggest small price to pay for having such love in our homes.

Although dog and cat lovers are usually always very devoted to their pets, it is nearly always assumed that the love we have for our pets is all that they need to sustain them. This is not always the case as some times it helps if we learn to emotionally and mentally interact with them. This is easily achieved through a simple method of *Meditating with your Pet* in the following way.

THINKING AND MEDITATING WITH YOUR PET

Most pet lovers will agree that our pets speak to us, and the majority of us understand exactly what they are saying. The pet lover who gets so frustrated simply because they don't understand what their pet is trying to say, have not really taken the trouble to learn their pet's language, which is completely different to ours. There are in fact so many things about your pet's true character that you do not see. Most people tend to take their pets for granted, and often wrongly assume – simply because they use a completely different system of communication – that their cat or dog cannot 'speak'. The frequency of an animal's mind is much higher than ours and, being unencumbered by those things that cause us so much stress and anxiety, there is far greater clarity in the reception and transmission of their thought processes. So through carefully attuning your mind to your pet's vibrations you can learn to talk to it, and with practice you may in fact become quite proficient at understanding exactly how it is feeling and what it is trying to say.

Let us take a look at a few extremely effective ways of how to make that 'connection' with your pet.

PET ATTUNEMENT MEDITATION NUMBER I

- *Sit comfortably beside your pet, either on the floor or on the sofa.*
- *With your eyes closed gently stroke your pet, feeling the warmth of its fur between your fingertips.*
- *Whilst you are doing this mentally reassure your pet of your love for it.*
- *Feel a deep spiritual bond with your pet, and be conscious of its love and devotion for you.*
- *Become totally relaxed, allowing your breathing to be nice and rhythmical, slow and deep.*
- *Now, in your mind's eye, see an intense pink light passing from your heart to your pet, and mentally see your pet surrounded by that pink light and glowing with it.*
- *Still stroking your pet, imagine that it is leading you through an archway of intense golden light. Follow it and see yourself emerging into a spacious hall with a glass-domed ceiling.*
- *Look up at the glass dome, and see that it is translucent, like mother of pearl.*
- *Around you the walls of the hall appear to shimmer with many different colours and there is a sweet fragrance in the air.*
- *Mentally see the light cascading down through the glass-domed ceiling, breaking up into a myriad of colours as it falls into the centre of the hall, forming a pool of sparkling light there.*
- *Walk with your pet until you reach the pool of light and stand there for a few moments. It is important to maintain the imagery and to mentally see your pet with you all the time. Do not allow your thoughts to drift from the exercise even for one moment.*
- *At this point you should begin to feel your pet becoming slightly*

agitated as it relaxes with you. This means you are beginning to make a connection with it, and your energies are beginning to interact.

- Feel totally at-one with your pet, and feel that you are both completely enveloped in a kaleidoscope of colours, shades and mixtures.

- Now, allow that imagery to slowly dissolve, and then bring your attention back to your pet relaxing with you, and re-establish the beam of intense pink light streaming from your heart and surrounding your pet.

- You should now sense your pet responding to this imagery, and it may make an effort to rise and move away from you.

- Send it a mental request, either to remain with you or perhaps to go to a specific room in the house. Tell it to do whatever you want it to. If the connection has been fully established between you and your pet, it should react almost immediately. If it doesn't respond this time you should not give up. Sometimes it takes three or four attempts before the cat or dog takes notice of what you are thinking. Remember, it is a scientific fact that both dogs and cats think in pictures, and so you should do the same. Should your request be for your pet to go to its water bowl, then you should mentally picture just that.

I suppose there is always the danger that a sceptic will dismiss the whole concept of the book purely on the basis that the above pet meditation exercise is a little farfetched. However, if you do have a dog or a cat then it is only fair that you give the exercise the benefit of the doubt and draw your conclusions later. It wouldn't really be fair to condemn it without giving it a try. So, give it a go and see what happens. If nothing else, it allows you to interact for a short time with your pet, and it is a bit of fun.

PET ATTUNEMENT MEDITATION NUMBER 2

- *As before, sit quietly beside your pet.*
- *With your eyes closed, place one hand gently on its head.*
- *Stroke its neck and head slowly with your fingertips. When you feel as though 'something' is passing from you to your pet, make every effort to establish this extremely important connection by sending it some simple mental commands, such as 'If you can hear me, stretch your body,' or perhaps 'Lick my hand'.*
- *At first there may be no positive response, as it may simply not be listening to you. Most dogs and cats have an extremely short attention span, so this part of the experiment might take quite a lot of patience on your part.*
- *It may be, though, that your pet responds immediately. This will depend on whether or not your little friend is in 'receive mode'.*
- *Once you have received a positive response a further mental command must be given – one that requires some physical effort from your pet.*
- *It might be a good idea to tell your pet to fetch an item from its toy box, or even for it to go to the door to be let out or to be taken for a walk. Whatever you ask your pet to do, you must say it in pictures. Once you have fully and positively established that telepathic connection with your furry friend you should have no problems at all understanding it and vice versa. Remember, though, as with all exercises of this nature, practice does make perfect and most certainly strengthens your telepathic relationship with your pet.*

CHAPTER NINE

THE HEALING PROCESS

Dogs and cats discharge their subtle healing energies while appearing to simply be expressing pleasure or when greeting other people. A dog will wag its tail and wiggle its bottom, while a cat will arch its back and purr, whilst raising its tail into an 'S' shape. Although most of us are oblivious to the release of this healing and perceive the animal as merely being friendly, the psychically inclined individual see the release of the subtle energy as shimmering vibrations of light, rather like electricity, completely surrounding the creature in a fan-like shape.

Although the cat discharges most of this force from its tail, the dog releases it predominantly from its head and sometimes its back. However, a dog possesses great amounts of the vitality in its rear end and the simple act of stroking its back down to its bottom precipitates a powerful release of the healing force. This process is extremely beneficial when one is feeling unwell or just a little under the weather so to speak. Not only does it have a calming effect upon the mind, but it also has the effect of anaesthetising the body to pain, simply by encouraging the release of endorphins (naturally occurring morphine like chemicals) in the brain.

Although the healing vitality of cats and dogs is to be found in the fur of both creatures, it is in fact more prevalent in the fur of the cat. Some schools of thought believe that there are nine degrees of animal healing vitality in the supersensual universe, and the cat is the only creature on the planet whose fur contains these nine degrees. Hence the saying, *'a cat has nine lives.'*

The subtle healing force is not peculiar to the animal kingdom alone. On the contrary, some humans possess it in great amounts, and these people have the ability to heal through the laying on of hands. As some people have the unusual ability to uplift us when we are feeling low or under the weather, so too do cats and dogs possess the same abilities.

Cats are able to transmute this vitality into a potent force and as a result they nearly always seem able to evade death when they find themselves in the most dangerous and precarious situations. I am of course referring to the metaphysical or spiritual aspects of a feline, and it is not therefore a theory that would be easily accepted by sceptics or conventional science.

The highly volatile nature of a cat's healing vitality is a key reason for its adversity to water. Placing a cat in water is like placing two opposing magnetic forces together. The same effect is achieved by simply breathing rhythmically for a few moments, visualising streams of intense white light passing through your nostrils, and then down into your fingertips. Then, blow into your fingertips, before shaking them vigorously, from tail to head, along your cat's back. Your cat will immediately arch its back, its tail will rise into the familiar 'S' shape, and it will then move as quickly away from you as possible.

This is yet another way of demonstrating the projection of your vitality into your cat. It has its own supply and so doesn't need yours; it's as simple as that. Although quite uncomfortable, it is harmless. The reaction is the result of the interaction of two opposing forces which, quite obviously your cat finds extremely unpleasant, but will frequently come back for more. In fact, your cat will find the unpleasant process quite intriguing. Because a dog's energies are not as vibrant, they will always find the experience quite pleasant, and will always express their pleasure sometimes by rolling onto their back. In fact, this is an extremely effective way of calming a dog down when it is hyperactive.

TRY THIS ON YOUR DOG:
This is an extremely effective tonic when your dog is not too

well. For this experiment you will need either a piece of muslin or linen, whichever is convenient.

- *When your dog is lying quietly, sit on the floor beside it, and place the small piece of cloth gently over the back of its head, taking care not to alarm it in anyway, as this will defeat the object of the experiment.*
- *Allow the cloth to remain there for a few moments before beginning. This is done primarily to ensure that your dog is not going to move position.*
- *Holding one hand across your dog's nose, to ensure it doesn't suddenly move its head, and then inhaling a complete breath, gently blow through the muslin and into the back of your dog's head.*
- *When your breath has been fully expelled, repeat the whole process again.*
- *After the breathing therapy has been done several times, sit back to note your dog's response to it. You should see that he or she has fallen into an even deeper sleep.*

Remember, this treatment can only be applied to dogs, and even then care should always be taken to ensure that your dog is not going to move suddenly or even snap at you. Even a placid dog can initially be shocked by this breathing treatment, and it may take a few minutes before the effects of it are really felt.

The breathing technique has been used for thousands of years, and is effective on humans as well as animals.

Families with more than one pet in the household will no doubt find that the healing power is far greater than with one dog or cat. Cats make a house serene and very peaceful, whilst dogs charge the atmosphere often making their owners feel fairly energetic. Although there may be a psychological explanation for this, the metaphysical implications are more obvious, certainly from a psychic's point of you.

When the energies of more than one dog living with a family are compatible, the animals will often relax in a huddle. (This behaviour is especially pronounced if there are multiple dogs in a home.) Their combined energies create a sort of powerful 'Healing Battery' giving off incredible heat, both physically and psychically. Anyone in the house suffering from arthritis or some other painful or inflammatory condition will derive great benefit from the healing force – without realising that it has anything whatsoever to do with the hairy huddle in front of the fire. It is now a scientific fact that dogs can definitely ease pain. In fact, the effects dogs have on the human organism are quite astounding, and today researchers are discovering even more facts about the powers our pets exert over us.

Both dogs and cats in multi-animal households pass on the healing force to each other, and when one of the group is feeling unwell it may move close to one of the other animals, in an effort to have its low levels of vitality restored. Animals are natural healers and only have their levels of vitality depleted either when they are unwell, or when they have been injured. In the latter case it is shock, a condition that often follows an injury, which causes a spontaneous loss of vitality in the animal.

Sickness creates a subtle fragrance that is perceptible to dogs and cats. The degree of fragrance informs them about the seriousness of the illness. Cats, especially, like to cuddle close to their sick owner and they most certainly contribute a lot towards his or her recovery. Although it is a known fact that cats like heat, and so are therefore attracted to the heat of a person's body when there is a fever, they also do this in an asserted effort to encourage the invalid's recovery.

Although the majority of veterinary surgeons I interviewed during the writing of this book fully understood and accepted the concept of animal healing, there was surprisingly a minority who dismissed it all as poppycock. I am quite sure that the marked differences in their opinions were also a measure of their different sensitivities towards animals as a whole. This does not in any way reflect on their abilities as veterinary surgeons, as much as it does on the way they perceive animals.

CHAPTER TEN

WAYS TO TREAT YOUR SICK PET

Most dog owners are so attuned to their pets that they know only too well when they are under the weather. You can encourage the healing process by stimulating its own powerful healing energies through the use of a number of different treatments. However, although the more serious conditions may necessitate a visit to the vet, the following treatments will complement the prescribed medication, thereby facilitating recovery.

TECHNIQUE ONE

- *Place your dog in a comfortable position which enables you to gain easy access to its spine. Use your right hand, with the fingers loosely outstretched, and simply shake your fingers quickly and energetically whilst moving your hand slowly down your dog's spine – from the base of the skull to the tip of the tail.*
- *Repeat this process, over and over, for five minutes, occasionally pausing to blow warm air into your fingertips, (as we did in a previous exercise,) and try to imagine that you are infusing your fingers with a powerful white energy. In fact, see this energy vividly in your mind, passing from your mouth to your fingertips, and then being transferred to your dog during the healing process. Try to feel your fingers almost alive with vitality.*
- *Next, simply stroke your dog slowly along the spine, following the same route as before, to encourage the movement of the healing force. Once you have completed the exercise you should see your dog become relaxed and probably go to sleep. When it wakes up you should see a marked difference in its whole demeanour.*

TECHNIQUE TWO

This technique is similar to one shown in an earlier chapter, only this time the treatment is applied all over the body.

- *As before you will need a piece of muslin or linen, whichever is at hand. Although the cloth encourages the healing process, it is also used in the interests of hygiene regardless of how clean your dog happens to be.*
- *As before, blow gently through the cloth into the top of your dog's head. Remain in this spot for a few minutes, as this helps to establish the healing process.*
- *Then remove the cloth and rub the area softly with your fingertips, primarily to encourage the movement of energy. You should find that the more you apply the treatment, the easier it will be.*
- *Next, move the cloth to the base of the skull and gently blow through it for a few moments. Again, rub the area gently to facilitate the healing.*
- *Continue this blowing technique along the route of your dog's spine, taking great care not to disturb it, and then concluding at the base, just before the tail.*
- *It is a good idea to use white cloth during the treatment as the white helps to retain the warmth created by the blowing, and this warmth is essential in the precipitation of the healing vitality. Because dogs have so much vitality in their bodies, the blowing process is extremely effective in encouraging its own healing reserves to fully recover.*

As I have previously stated, this technique is also beneficial to humans, particularly in those cases involving a great deal of pain.

TECHNIQUE THREE

The same 'blowing' treatment may be applied using different coloured pieces of cloth depending on the degree and nature of the illness.

- **RED LINEN** *will infuse the vitality from your breath with strength and power. It is extremely beneficial in the healing of blood conditions and for lifting feelings of lethargy. It will also help to alleviate pain in the joints.*
- **ORANGE LINEN** *is extremely effective where there are digestive problems, or when there is a lack of appetite accompanied perhaps by tiredness.*
- **YELLOW LINEN** *will aid the stimulation of the major glands and organs of the body and is extremely beneficial in the healing of kidney or urinary problems.*
- **GREEN LINEN** *has a remarkable effect upon the heart and will also aid the recovery from emotional or psychological trauma.*
- **BLUE LINEN** *will aid the process of relaxation and will also help to promote equilibrium between the body, mind and spirit. In fact, blue is one of the most powerful healing colours effective on most health problems.*
- **INDIGO LINEN** *seems to have a general toning effect upon the body and the mind. It is also very beneficial in encouraging recovery from serious illness.*
- **VIOLET LINEN** *tends to have a holistic effect upon the whole body and is extremely effective in the treatment of cancerous conditions.*

Remember, though, it is not the linen that does the healing, as much as the infusion of the colour and the vitality from your own body. Once the breath reaches the coloured linen, your vitality immediately becomes infused with the appropriate colour vibrations, the combination of which produces a powerful effect upon the condition you are treating.

Although I intended this book to be primarily concerned with the healing powers possessed by animals, it is equally important to understand the ways in which these powers can actually be used to heal the animals themselves when they are ill. Your pets are little powerhouses on four legs, and they possess the ability not only to heal you, but also to heal themselves.

TECHNIQUE FOUR

- *Dogs more than cats appear to respond to the healing vibrations of colour, and certain colours may be used around your pet to encourage the healing of specific illnesses. For example ,should your dog be too hyperactive, and forever on the go, put a pink sheet or cover on its bed. Pink is an extremely calming colour and its vibrations will also promote restful sleep.*

- *If your pet is suffering from a high temperature, give it a blue blanket to sleep on. The vibrations of the colour blue will help to reduce the temperature and, as your pet is not susceptible to suggestion, there can be no question of a placebo effect. Colour treatment can be quite effective, and in a lot of cases extremely powerful. In fact, colour healing has been used for thousands of years, and in ancient Egypt was the most popular treatment employed by the physicians in the royal palaces. As I have previously explained, different coloured muslin would be stretched across an opening to allow the sun's rays to filter through onto the patient. This therapy was used to treat all maladies of both the body and the mind with great success.*

- *An elderly dog who is perhaps suffering from a tired or diseased heart will quite often benefit from the treatment involving the colours green and blue. Allow your pet to rest for a while on a green cover or sheet bathed, if possible, in a green light. Then change the cover to a blue one, bathing your dog in a blue light. Of course, this treatment must be applied over a number of weeks, in order to obtain the desired results.*

- *Just as one would expect the colour blue to reduce a higher than normal temperature, the colour red will help to raise it when your pet is suffering from a chill and has a low temperature. Allow your little invalid to rest for half an hour or so on a red cover, and bathe it in a red light for just fifteen minutes. Results should be achieved quickly with this colour, because red vibrations carry a great deal of energy and has a tendency to create a lot of heat in a physical organism. It is also an extremely effective colour in the healing of arthritis.*

- *Generally speaking yellow is a stimulating colour and can be very effective when treating health conditions that result in fatigue and lethargy. But yellow is also useful when treating stomach, bowel or kidney conditions. Treatments using the yellow vibration will be greatly strengthened when concluded with a short period of green, for this is the colour of harmony and equilibrium. Just one cautionary note: because of the stimulating vibrations of yellow, treatment with this colour should be kept to a minimum, and care taken not to over-saturate the system with its vibrations.*

- *Animals suffering from terminal illnesses can often have their pain and discomfort reduced greatly by treating them with the colours purple and blue. As before, allow your pet to lie on a bed of purple for 30 minutes and if possible bathe it in a blue light for a further 15 minutes. Then reverse the process and allow your pet to rest on a bed of blue to be bathed if possible in a purple light. This treatment will not cure the condition but it will certainly help to alleviate and ease the suffering.*

Dogs are naturally drawn to nature and therefore benefit from, and greatly appreciate, a regular walk in the countryside or park. Nature's colours are naturally so important to the Animal Kingdom and the colour green in particular is vital to a dog's mental and emotional equilibrium. Just to feel the cool grass beneath its paws is a tonic in itself. Dogs love to roll over on the grass – but it also connects them to the earth and helps their systems to be recharged with energy and the natural vitality of the planet. In fact, we humans could learn a great deal from dogs, who seem to know exactly what to do, and how to do it, to restore their energies by 'tapping-in' so to speak, to the universal reservoir of vitality and power.

My Old English Sheepdog, Harry, used to love to roll over in the freshly dug earth of the vegetable patch, to my sheer horror and his delight. Then he would lie flat out and motionless in it imbibing the energy of the whole dirty process, for anything up to 20 minutes and sometimes longer, after which time he would demonstrate an energetic marathon running around the garden. It was obvious that his sojourn in the vegetable patch did more for him than just cool him down in warm weather. To psychically see Harry when he emerged from the broccoli stems was quite a sight to behold. Sparks of electricity would appear to fly off him in all directions and he would almost glow with power. Holding him close and giving him a cuddle at that time was quite invigorating, as the vitality he had created would pass from him to me rather like a surge of electricity. In fact, it made me feel as though I was plugged into an electrical generator.

Like humans, animals derive most of their vitality from the air and the sunlight. Water tends to be an excellent conductor of the vitality necessary for the maintenance of the health in the physical body. Water is also a cleansing agent and has a purifying effect upon the organs of the body and the blood. Water may also be infused with a specific healing colour ray with the following procedure. This technique can also be used in the treatment of human ailments, but animals somehow respond to it a lot quicker.

EXERCISE FIVE

- *For this treatment you will need to obtain a number of sheets of A4 acetate, in as many different colours as possible. Simply make each piece into a tube, by either Sellotaping or stapling them, ensuring that they are large enough to fit over a glass tumbler. Alternatively, coloured glass tumblers may be used.*
- *The object here is to filter the natural vitality coming into the*

water from the sunlight, and by introducing a specific colour ray into the process, you thus increase the water's vitality.

- *Place the appropriate filter over a glass of water, which should then be placed on a window ledge in the bright sunlight, preferably outdoors.*

- *Leave the tumbler exposed to the sunlight for at least an hour. After that time, pour the water from one tumbler into another, backwards and forwards, over and over again, until the water almost comes 'alive'. Once the water has been revitalised, pour it into your dog's bowl. It is a good idea to prepare a few tumblers so that there is enough charged water for a few doses. Should the water remain in the bowl for any length of time, either revitalise it or replace it with a fresh tumbler.*

- *When using the coloured filters it is important to use your imagination and instinctively select the appropriate colours. I have already said that red is a powerful colour that tends to create heat in the physical body. It will help to raise a temperature when it is low, but it will also give energy to your pet when it is lethargic. Blue is quite the opposite and will lower the temperature when it is high. Water charged with a blue filter will also calm the nerves when there is some anxiety or hyperactivity.*

At the beginning of this book I said that *'A cuddle a day keeps the doctor away.'* I would now like to add to that *'A cuddle a day also keeps the vet away.'*

Cuddling or stroking your dog as a show of affection releases a lot more than physical warmth. There is definitely a more subtle process at work here – an exchange of energy that has the power to heal human illnesses of both the body and the mind and can also help to sustain and prolong the life of both the human and the pet.

CHAPTER ELEVEN

YOUR PET AFTER DEATH

There is little doubt that once a pet has well and truly established itself in the home it becomes one of the family. Having a furry presence in the house contributes something quite special to the overall atmosphere. Only an animal lover can be privy to those almost sacred feelings that are passed on to anyone who belongs to this elite group of 'animal people'.

This will no doubt sound quite ridiculous to those who do not love animals and that is exactly the point I am trying to make. Once your pet captures your heart some sort of magical transformation takes place in the emotions, and life, believe me, can never be the same again.

Dog and cat lovers seem to undergo some sort of secret initiation into the club of *silly talk,* in which *'walkies...din-dins...Who's mummy's little baby?'* are commonplace language. Of course our faithful little friends understand every single word.

Little wonder then when the inevitable happens, and that little furry presence dies, either through age, illness, or the worst scenario – a car accident – the grief seems nearly always as painful and unbearable as that of losing any other member of the family. In fact, to some people it is quite often worse and produces a devastating effect upon the whole of the family. The majority of animal lovers have, at some time, experienced the loss of a pet, and are only too familiar with that horrible silent emptiness that pervades the house!

Coming to terms with the loss of a pet can be extremely difficult, and for an elderly person living alone, painfully sad, as they bid farewell to a constant, loving companion. 'Replacing' a pet, or even just thinking of 'replacing' it generates unbearable feelings of guilt. It is commonly felt that to replace a pet with another one, even some considerable time after their death, would be disloyal, and would cause some sadness and jealousy to the pet that has died. It is often strongly believed that the little creature may be looking on from that part of the *Spiritual Universe* where animals go to when they die.

But where do animals go to when they die? Do they even have souls? If they do have souls do they go to the same place as humans? Is there a heaven and hell for animals? Do they continue living in the same way as humans in some sort of an afterlife?

Many Christian fundamentalists would find it quite offensive at the mere suggestion that animals have souls and live on after death. This might be to salve their consciences about the fact that they allow animals to be killed for their own consumption! Nonetheless, there has been far too much evidence to support the fact that animals survive bodily death in exactly the same way as humans, and that they do live on in their own particular place in the Spirit World.

When your pet's *Spiritual Essence* is released at death, it gravitates towards that *sphere of light* where all animals reside. Strictly speaking, there are no evil animals and therefore no plane of existence that could in any way be defined as 'Hell'.

The aggressive creature does not choose to be aggressive and has no control over its aggression. Unlike the human the animal does not possess a conscience, at least not in the same way as the conscience of a human, so it therefore cannot be considered guilty of any misdeed. Although it must be said that some domestic animals do exhibit some form of rudimentary conscience, but even these cannot be held responsible for their actions when they show a sudden outburst of aggression.

All creatures great and small do live on beyond death, and there have been innumerable accounts where a pet has visited its grieving owner from beyond the grave.

Although the more advanced animals retain their individual

personalities beyond death, their evolutionary processes continue in the collective sense. All animals evolve spiritually, emotionally and intellectually through the group soul. It was once said, *Man knows; the animal knows; but man knows that he knows, simply because he has an intellect and the animal does not!* I am quite certain that this ancient precept would not stand up today as much as it did when it was first expounded. Researchers have concluded that animals have a rudimentary form of intelligence that enables them to learn complicated tasks and routines. Although a dog may not be *aware* of itself in the same way that we are aware of ourselves, it still possesses an *awareness* that is much sharper and more efficient than human awareness.

When my wife's mother passed away six years ago we inherited Pesi her pussycat. Pesi was a black and white pussycat with an extremely loving nature. She was very demonstrative with her feelings and knew exactly when one of us was not feeling too well. She was clingy and always welcomed a cuddle. In fact, she divided her love equally between my wife and me, and so when her eighteen years caught up with her, and we knew that we would soon have to say goodbye to her, we were understandably devastated. Eventually, Pesi came to each one of us in turn just to say 'goodbye,' and then she went upstairs to die. As with all cats she wanted to be in a dark corner alone, and so she crawled under the bed. My wife sat on the floor on one side of the bed, and I sat on the other. Although Pesi was only semi-conscious, every so often she would struggle to raise her head, first to look at my wife, and then to look at me, I suppose to make certain we were there. When the end eventually came, Pesi arched her back, turned to look at us in turn, I think to say her final farewell, and then she lay down still and lifeless. Pesi was a beautiful cat who we both miss so much. She used to love to sit on the window ledge in our bedroom, watching the different birds flying over the estuary, and then when she'd had enough, she would jump onto our bed and snuggle in. Pesi died three years ago now, and even today we frequently glimpse her walking around the house. Some mornings we glimpse her briefly sitting on the window ledge watching the birds as she always did, and then feel her weight as she jumps on the bed to snuggle in between us. I suppose all cat owners say the same thing, but Pesi was a very special and beautiful pussycat and a gentle creature with no aggression at all. It is a comforting thought to know that she is still around us, going about her daily routine in much the same way as she did when she was still alive.

Apart from wanting to share this story of Pesi with you, I also told it to explain the two very different phenomena of our *pet's return*, both which prove beyond a shadow of doubt that animals most definitely possess the same spiritual qualities as humans and more.

Any strong emotion discharged either by human or animal, is impregnated into the subtle structure of the bricks and mortar of a building. In the same way that audio and video tapes are coated with an electro-magnetic substance enabling sounds and images to be recorded, so too is there an electro-magnetic substance in the atmosphere, capable of capturing emotionally charged images and sounds of things that have passed. These images may be replayed for hundreds of years, and although they appear as vivid, ghostly apparitions, they are no more than photographic images in the atmosphere. That is only one explanation for our pet's return. Even though with this particular phenomenon it is no more than just like watching old video footage on a television screen, it only happens because the animal or person you see has been extremely happy in that location, and although the apparition is just a ghostly image with absolutely no awareness, their appearance is most certainly a demonstration of love.

The second phenomenon is when your pet appears to you and even responds to your voice. There are many cases where pets have returned to their grieving owners, and have even allowed them to physically make contact. Of course, with this phenomenon the ghostly visitor only returns occasionally. With the *photographic image* phenomenon, it can occur as frequently as your grief requires it. In the case of our pussycat Pesi, it was most definitely her spirit that returned to the home she loved. She responded to us with her usual meow and purr before she disappeared. Unfortunately, Pesi does not call to see us as frequently now; and I can only assume that even though we still miss, she now knows that we are over the worst of our grief.

Ridiculous as it may sound to some people, the family pet feels a sense of responsibility towards its owner, especially when it has been an integral part of an extremely loving relationship. And it is this sense of responsibility and concern which draws it back to the family after it has died.

One of the most common experiences pet owners have when their cat or dog dies, is to continue to 'feel' them around the home. In a lot of cases they may even be fleetingly seen sitting on their favourite chair, or perhaps curled up in their favourite corner. These experiences transcend the bounds of coincidence and imagination because far too many people have had astoundingly similar experiences.

Even though the owner may not always be aware of the furry creature's presence, just being around the home allows the pet to continue its own personal development, as well as enabling it to further enjoy those wonderful waves of love created by the family. This love is so important for the spiritual evolution of animals and without it the animal kingdom as a whole would be unable to function and grow.

In the Great Spiritual Universe the various species of animals occupy their own individual stratum of existence, but the same spiritual body that unifies the whole of creation unifies all animals into one powerful spiritual unit. These animal planes of existence are tended by a group of highly evolved souls who together have sole charge over the Animal Kingdom. Very few of these exalted beings have ever experienced a physical existence and those amongst them who have, have become known on earth for their kindly and compassionate works towards animals. Saint Francis, amongst many others, is one such being and his name is now synonymous with the care and love of animals.

A dog or cat who has integrated into family life and has become attuned to, and very much a part of the family, has usually evolved an almost human-like intelligence and knowing nature. It needs therefore to come back often from the spirit world, not only to imbibe the family love and to make quite sure that everything and everyone is alright, but also to offer some reassurance to the family of their own continued existence after death. An animal that has been treated with love and kindness will never forget, and will always take every opportunity to return to those who have given it so much love.

On the other hand, animals that have been treated cruelly never bear any malice or seek revenge on those who have inflicted so much pain and misery upon them. The perpetrators of such cruelty towards innocent creatures have a flaw in their spiritual natures and are eventually punished by their own cruelty. Nothing in creation ever passes by unnoticed, for the same spiritual laws that operate in the Great Spiritual Universe are also in constant operation in the physical world and work primarily under the umbrella of the *Laws of Attraction.*

All animals on earth are the ambassadors and representatives of those spiritual beings who silently and relentlessly watch over and guide mankind. .

It may or may not come as a great surprise to pet owners to learn that they have an angel in their home. Believe me, *not all angels have wings.* If you truly love your pet you will understand exactly what I mean.

CHAPTER TWELVE

DO ANIMALS REINCARNATE?

Although the Doctrine of Reincarnation has for thousands of years been an integral part of all Eastern traditions, Christian teachings totally reject the concept as being offensive. Nonetheless, today with the growing interest in New Age philosophies, devotees of the concept of Reincarnation have increased tenfold, causing the integration of many of the ancient traditions into the western way of thinking. Although some schools of esoteric thought accept *transmigration* (humans reborn into the bodies of animals) as an integral part of reincarnation, this concept is totally dismissed by the majority of devotees of reincarnation. However, what is accepted by the majority of followers of reincarnation is the actual process of the rebirth of animals into the bodies of other animals. This seems to me to be a fair exchange, and makes far more sense than humans being subjected to rebirth in the bodies of animals, which is quite difficult to understand. Although sceptics would probably view the very suggestion of this as being a little more than bizarre, the evidence to support it is quite astounding with stories of dogs and cats actually returning to their grieving owners in the bodies of other loving animals.

Those creatures who live alongside humans are born with a special mission to fulfil. Each one is spiritually linked to the others of its species, collectively forming the group soul. Therefore, once each creature has reached a specific phase in its spiritual evolutionary development, the whole group is then recalled to be subjected thereafter to the process of reincarnation.

As I have already stated above, the doctrine of rebirth forms an integral part of some religious and philosophical teachings, especially Buddhism. However, reincarnation of the Animal Kingdom is very different, and far more complex, than that of humans.

Animals in Eastern traditions are often used as 'vehicles of transgression'. For example, man may be reborn into the body of an animal should he perform some grave misdeed, or perhaps be cruel to an animal or even delight in killing animals unnecessarily. The concept of 'Transmigration of Souls', being reincarnated into the body of an animal as a punishment for our sins, is a belief embraced by many Eastern cultures.

In the process of rebirth animals are mostly born in groups and not always as the same breed of their species. Collectively they make up the group soul that works towards the fuller development of the Animal Kingdom as a whole. The group soul is continued into life, where although separated in a physical sense, it is believed they maintain a telepathic connection.

Should a domesticated animal form a close bond with a human they may disconnect from the group, at least for a short while, in order to continue and deepen its relationship with the owner in a different body. Such are the connections between some pets and their owners that they are reborn immediately after death. This is very often in an asserted effort to comfort the grieving family through the guise of another creature. When this happens, the circumstance will always present itself to enable the reincarnated pet to once again infiltrate the family to live happily with them as before.

This may sound even more bizarre to some grieving pet owners who affirm that 'No *other dog/cat could ever take her place*' but you don't have to look for another dog or cat to replace the one you have lost, as when the time is right *it* will most definitely find you. It seems to be the general consensus of opinion amongst the devotees of animal reincarnation that this is the way it all actually works.

There was the case of the elderly lady whose daughter

brought her a young Border Collie after her own 17 year old mongrel had died. Although the very thought of replacing her loyal companion, Major, brought tears to her eyes, she agreed, if only to pacify her daughter's concern. Although the Border Collie had a sweet and loving nature, Mary Roberts had already made up her mind that she was not going to keep the little doggy for any longer than two weeks. Her mind was made up and that was that! However, Mary began slowly to change her mind when she noticed the Border Collie seemed to be familiar with its new surroundings, and even came to her when she accidentally called it 'Major'. Her new lodger would even go to the cupboard where she used to keep Major's biscuits and toys. But it wasn't until Mary's favourite programme came on the television that she was convinced Major and the new doggy were one and the same. As soon as he heard the programme's theme tune the little Border Collie began to bark with delight at the television, just like Major used to. That was three years ago and the little doggy is still with Mary. She was so certain that Major had come back to her in the new dog that she even called him Major.

This is just one of many very similar stories that have convinced both dog and cat lovers that their pets have returned to them in the body of another creature.

CHAPTER THIRTEEN

THE HOLY PRESENCE

If the purpose of man's sojourn in this world is that he may aspire to God-like status, then no doubt dogs and cats have attained such exalted heights already.

All through this book I have suggested that our pets can be, and very often are, extremely manipulative, and most, if not all of them, do possess the knowledge of exactly what power they have over us. But in my exploration of the healing powers of animals, and in particular dogs, I have come to believe that they are the nomadic disciples of some holy power to which we are not privy – at least at present.

As we have discussed previously, losing a dog member of the family to many people is just like losing any other member of the family. The grieving process is very often such that the statement 'No other dog will ever replace him. I'll never get another one,' is said with feeling and finality. In fact, most dogs exhibit a huge presence around the home. Not only are they able to give that all-essential love to their owners, particularly when he or she is unwell, but the pet of the family somehow possesses the power to encourage that person to fight whatever malady has befallen them.

I heard about such a case from an elderly lady whose sister had died recently from a gangrenous condition that eventually spread throughout her whole body. The lady in question was in her early eighties, and had lived alone with her 14 year-old mongrel Michael, since her husband had died 10 years before.

It seems that, unknown to anyone, she had been desperately ill for at least two years, but had been afraid to seek medical attention for fear that her constant companion, Michael, would have to be put to sleep on her admittance to hospital. Sadly, Michael died suddenly of heart failure, allowing her owner to seek treatment in hospital. Unfortunately, by this time her condition was so extensive that she herself died only two days later.

This in fact is a classic case of the power our pets exert over us by the love they encourage us to give them. They undoubtedly have an extremely powerful psychological effect upon our lives, and those who do not like animals are, sadly, greatly missing out on something quite wonderful.

Whatever magic it is that they are able to weave around us, dogs and cats know full well what they are doing. Their mischief, cheek and curiosity culminate into an inimitable personality peculiar to that creature alone. It makes sense then that the owner of a cat or dog in whose relationship there is a very special bond will always be able to identify their pet from a line up of similar creatures.

There is no great mystery or surprise either in the story of the cat who disappeared just before its owners moved home from the north of England, to live in Scotland. This amazing pet somehow found them, after travelling the great distance on foot (or I should say on paw), to arrive miraculously at their front door, somewhat exhausted, two weeks later.

One elderly and overweight cat was apparently so fed up with being subjected to all sorts of (necessary) veterinary treatment that it left home, seemingly to punish its elderly owner. However, the cat returned six months later, half the size it had been, but apparently a lot healthier. Cat and owner now have an understanding – she always asks her cat's permission before taking him along to the vet, and she insists that her cat fully understands every word she is saying.

There is no doubt that the person who has been brought up with animals is emotionally different from the one who has not. Whether or not you accept the presence of a metaphysical healing force where animals are concerned, matters very little. The truth is that animals great and small do pass on something to us, and this 'something', whatever one chooses to call it, is of great benefit to our emotional and mental equilibrium. The long-term effects of this on our physical health can be quite profound.

Catching sight of a rabbit, a squirrel, or even a weasel running across our path seems to cause the movement of chemicals in the brain, precipitating the emotions, and even the hardest of people cannot fail to be affected by such an experience.

It is one of life's great mysteries though how anyone can end the life of a wild creature in the name of sport, without the slightest feeling of guilt or sadness. Animals have to be tolerant with us, and they cannot in any way protest about all the inhumane things that we impose upon them. Of one thing I am quite certain, and that is that even the gentlest of animals are not given the opportunities that some of the wickedest, cruellest humans are given; and although the Animal Kingdom appears now to have a louder voice speaking on its behalf, the dreadful offences against them still continue.

Quite apart from their wonderful and endearing value as family pets, dogs are in fact invaluable in many other ways: There are over 4,000 guide dogs for the blind in Britain, and over 100 extremely clever dogs trained especially to help the disabled around the home, and generally to make their lives a little easier. There are dogs trained to act as 'ears' for those whose hearing is impaired. They can fetch the post, bring in the milk, turn on the lights, and retrieve things from the fridge or cupboard. Dogs are now specially trained to search not only for drugs or bombs but also for missing or injured people and of course 'sniffer' dogs who work with the police, army and rescue services. The list of things dogs are trained to do is endless, and there is very little doubt that more things will come to light in the future.

The acute sensitivity possessed by both cats and dogs enables them to know in advance when there is going to be an earthquake, or even when a volcano is going to erupt. Of course, there is also the tradition of taking canaries down mine shafts to test for gas, or watching the behaviour animals exhibit if a house is haunted.

As stated in a previous chapter, the psychic abilities of both dogs and cats enable them to monitor molecular changes in the atmosphere around them, allowing them to know about potentially devastating natural occurrences, often days in advance. Little wonder why dogs and cats are special and very important to us humans.

Dogs are not just cuddly ornamental creatures to have around the home, for they can also be useful in detecting an approaching illness or even an epileptic seizure, enabling the sufferer to take appropriate measures long before it actually happens. Some dogs are now being trained especially to watch over severe epilepsy sufferers.

The auditory faculties of a cat are so acute that our human hearing is nothing in comparison. The cat can register sound frequencies up to 65khz, whereas we can only register frequencies up to 20khz. A cat's hearing is so sharp that it can *home-in* to, and even recognise, its owner's footsteps from several hundred feet away.

Dogs, it would seem, can register sounds of 35,000 vibrations per second, and a cat 25,000 vibrations per second, in comparison to a human's 20,000 per second.

Science today recognises the importance and therapeutic value of having a pet, and it is now known that having a cat or dog around the home lessens one's susceptibility to most minor ailments such as headaches, depression, arthritis and even backache.

So a cuddle from your pet every day definitely keeps the doctor away. Tests have in fact shown that simply stroking your dog or cat helps to normalise blood pressure, and can also help to lower stress levels. As I have repeatedly pointed out in the pages of this book, so much more can be achieved simply by having animals around the home. How privileged we are to share this planet with the Animal Kingdom.

We must then consider that the Animal Kingdom as a whole is a constant reminder to us of all those things that we should be and all those things that one day we could be.

Remember also that the animals you have with you in your home are most certainly *Angels here on earth to help us, guide us and heal our wounds.*

CHAPTER FOURTEEN

MORE DOGS NOT TO BE SNIFFED AT

Although dogs have always been considered man's best friend, with the extraordinary ability to uplift its owner's spirits when he or she is feeling a little under the weather, today the medical world is waking up to the fact that our pets contribute far more to our lives than previously thought. In 2003 an article was featured in The Sunday Express entitled, *THE DOGS WHO CAN SNIFF OUT CANCER*. And so it is confirmed, as well as detecting disastrous situations dogs can also sniff out disease. Some medical doctors believe so much in the 'sniffing' powers of dogs that they compromised their professional integrity by continuing their research regardless of how much criticism they received from their peers. One such doctor in Russia gave up his well paid job in biological research to continue his studies of the healing powers of animals, with a particular curiosity about the way that dogs can 'sniff' disease in human beings.

It has even been suggested that one day every hospital and doctor's surgeries will have a specially trained dog to sniff disease where conventional diagnostic medicine fails.

Another amazing breakthrough in the controversial field of 'sniffer' dogs is their ability now to sniff breast and prostate cancer when its difficult to diagnose.

Dr John Church who makes a study of the phenomenon of sniffer dogs commented, 'It has been well demonstrated that dogs can detect many illnesses. Dogs have detected skin cancer on their owners and I have personally seen a dog detect lung and breast cancer from samples of the breath.' Dr Church went on to say, 'What we don't know is how many cases a dog might miss. We can't take that risk with patients. We need large-scale research to establish dogs' hit rates. But one day, dogs might be used regularly in conjunction with other diagnostic tools.'

Cambridge University and Addenbrooke's hospital is seeking funding for a 12 month trial. The plan is to use Labradors and Alsatians to diagnose prostate cancer, which as we know kills more men than any other disease except lung cancer. Dr Barbara Sommerville is leading the research, and she said: 'We will train the dogs to distinguish the odour of urine from men with malignant prostate tumours, then present them with samples and measure their success rate.'

In the medical journal, The Lancet in 1989, Dr Hywel Williams and Dr Andrew Pembroke, two British doctors, first described dogs' abilities to detect cancer; a woman's malignant melanoma was diagnosed after her dog, a border collie/Doberman cross, kept sniffing a mole on her leg. The dog had shown no interest in any of other moles.

'The dog may have saved her owner's life by spurring her to seek medical advice while the mole was still at a non-invasive stage,' commented Dr Williams, now a professor at the University of Nottingham. A year later the two doctors reported another case of diagnosis, concerning a 66 year old man with what he thought was a patch of eczema on his leg. After his Labrador persistently sniffed the affected part of his leg, the man went to his doctor to have it looked at. The patch was removed and it was found to be cancerous.

It was this and other cases that prompted Florida-based dermatologist, Dr Armand Cognetta (mentioned in a previous chapter) to begin experimenting with his dog, a schnauzer named George, formerly a police dog.

George's success rate left no doubt that his diagnostic skills could in no way be described as chance. As a result of George's ability to 'sniff', a patient had several moles previously thought to be benign, removed from her body. These were found to be cancerous.

In San Francisco, a standard poodle named Shing Ling was also taught to detect lung and breast cancer by breath samples.

Dogs are now being trained to detect all manner of diseases in the human body. Some dogs bark others just stare, and some even push the patient towards a chair, particularly when an epileptic seizure is about to occur. It is thought that the dogs recognise multiple changes in the body such as breathing and muscle tone. The sniffer dog can even identify the slightest changes in body odour.

Fifty years ago, German scientist and dog expert Walter Neuhas did elaborate experiments on dogs' noses and concluded that their power is one million to 100 million times greater than that of human noses. No robot or machine is capable of doing what a dog's nose can do, which is why they are used to search for bombs, mines, drugs and even underground gas leaks and earthquake victims. Although sniffer machines are being developed, it is thought that these are very costly and may only be as good as the person who last serviced them.

There is very little doubt that dogs present much more than a furry, warm and playful personality; they are not only man's best friend, but they are capable of saving human lives, and in the future may even be an integral part of a hospital medical team.

There's no doubt at all that dogs are amazing creatures, and we are so much the better with them in our lives. I for one cannot even imagine what life would be like without either a dog or cat to share it with. They are truly angels without wings.

CHAPTER FIFTEEN

PET ASTROLOGY - BUT ALL FOR FUN

Whether or not you believe in astrology as a means of gleaning information about your future, the fact is that millions of people do believe to the extent that they won't make any decisions until they have checked the astrological forecast in the daily paper.Those who disregard astrology and view it generally as rubbish would probably dismiss this chapter completely. However, at the risk of discrediting the rest of this book I am going to explore the astrological status of your dog and cat, to enable you to have a better understanding of your pet's character, temperament and personality. After all, if astrology can be applied to you then why shouldn't it also be applied to your pet?

Over the last 15 years or so a whole new concept of pet psychology has evolved. Many now believe that animals – just like humans – are influenced by the movements and positioning of the planets in the heavens. In the same way that our moods, emotions and personalities differ according to the map of the heavens when we are born, animals too have very different characteristics, likes and fears according to their star sign.

I am not suggesting that you should check the daily astro-logical forecast for your pet to see how its day is going to go. What I am suggesting is that a little study of your pet's psychic and astrological profile may enable you to understand it even more, and will also help you to see exactly what lies behind the facade of the creature you think you know. Let us take the example of Cancerians. The insecurities and sensitivity often seen in the true Cancerian human are also seen in the Cancerian cat or dog, maybe with a very slight variation. The Cancerian person can be extremely emotional and very moody, but also quite communicative and very good with people. The cat or dog born under the astrological sign of Cancer desperately needs and thrives on love and affection. It needs a secure and stable home life, and plenty of interactions with humans. It loves to be stroked and cuddled and without these things it very quickly develops even more emotional insecurities and becomes depressed as a direct consequence. More Cancerian people than we realise possess addictive personalities and often become slaves to anything that pleases the senses. The Cancerian dog or cat can be just the same and may quite easily develop an obsessive nature. More than all this though, the Cancerian creature often exhibits one of the strongest personalities, and usually possesses the most effective ability to heal. The more it is allowed to interact with the family, the more healing it is able to release into the home. In fact, the Cancerian is extremely family orientated and loves to be around people. Remember though, I'm not talking about some nebulous feeling that affects us purely on a psychological level, but about a very potent force that has the power to affect healing in the human organism. Like humans, the creature born under the astrological sign of Cancer is the most psychic of all animals – it is the most receptive and the strongest transmitter of the healing force.

This is not to say though that animals born under other astro-logical signs do not have such abilities. On the contrary, all animals, regardless of when they were born, have their own special metaphysical abilities. I have chosen the Cancerian pet as an example, because in my opinion the creatures born under that astrological sign possess the most special qualities. In my experience though, the 'water' signs – Cancer, Pisces and Scorpio do appear to be able to transmute and transmit the healing force more effectively than any other astrological sign.

Of course, as any astrologer will tell you, the following astro-logical assessments are very general, and a proper chart needs to be drawn up before a detailed profile and forecast of the individual's life can be accurately made.

And so now let us turn our consideration to all 12 astrological signs and the way in which your pet is influenced and affected by the magnetic pull of the planets each day. Given this information you will then have a good idea of what exactly to look for in your pet, so that you can recognise and benefit from its particular qualities as well as its peculiarities.

ARIES DOG
ELEMENT FIRE

This creature can be quite laid back, and although a rather sensitive animal and one which will always respond to love and affection, it can be quite stubborn, and will certainly not do anything it doesn't want to do. It is quite an extremely strong sign, and even the female born under it can exhibit very strong masculine tendencies.

The dog born under the astrological sign of Aries often appears to be lost in thought and sometimes tends to live in its own little world. However, this is not always the case, as the Aries dog knows exactly how to relax, and has somehow evolved the ability to simply 'turn off' the power, so to speak.

The dog born under the astrological sign of Aries certainly likes comfort and once it has been allowed to curl up on the master's chair I am afraid that nothing whatsoever will persuade it to move without taking umbrage. Yes, the Aries dog knows how to sulk and has developed this to a fine art.

The healing powers discharged by this dog are quite extraordinarily strong and very good for those humans who lack confidence and are over sensitive.

ARIES CAT

This creature, unlike the dog, can be rather adventurous and is extremely nosy. It can be affectionate, but knows exactly when it has had enough. Although it is quite selective over the company it keeps, because of its likeable nature it is never without a collection of friends. This cat enjoys the comforts of home life, and although it likes to roam, it certainly knows when it is well off and so will always return to its home.

This cat's natural healing energies are extremely effective in encouraging the recovery of a distraught nervous person and helping the them back to good health.

The cat born under the astrological sign of Aries is far from lazy, and although it will always seem to be doing something, it may not be an early riser.

TAURUS DOG
ELEMENT EARTH

This creature possesses a healthy sense of fun and is perhaps one of the most practical of dogs. It likes pleasure and will go to extreme lengths to gratify its passions and desires. In saying this, the Taurus dog is quite old fashioned (if dogs can be old fashioned) and will always appear quite honest and very open.

The Taurus dog likes to over-indulge, sometimes carrying things to the extreme. If a dog can have a butterfly mind, then the Taurus dog has one. However, as with all Taurus personalities, this is a thoughtful, loving creature who is extremely faithful and very protective.

The dog born under the astrological sign of Taurus possesses extremely strong energies; just gently stroking its back will fill you with calmness and help to promote serenity and peace of mind. The energies emanating from this creature will also bring relief to those painful arthritic limbs.

On a more practical note, the Taurus dog is an extremely good listener, as far as dogs go anyway, and is usually very obedient.

TAURUS CAT

This creature can be extremely bossy, especially where humans are concerned, and is prone to sulking for unusually long periods! Its jealous nature may prevent it from interacting well with other animals.

However, the Taurus cat can also be quite sensual, and is extremely warm and affectionate.

Although as with all cats this creature is exceptionally clean in itself, it is perhaps not the tidiest of cats to have around the home.

The Taurus cat's healing abilities tend to be very vibrant and have the effect of anaesthetising the body to pain and anxiety. Its company is very calming on the mind and soul, and yet it tends to be selective about the company it keeps.

GEMINI DOG
ELEMENT AIR

The Gemini dog is full of character and knows exactly how to win hearts. Usually very kind by nature it quickly attunes itself to people's emotions. The Gemini dog is quite energetic and very boisterous, and with a lively personality it can be quite difficult to control. It is perhaps one of the most communicative of all astrological signs. Its charismatic nature may win hearts but also has a side which can be unpredictably moody, quite nervous and sometimes very unstable. Overall the Gemini dog has an extremely playful nature and has great difficulty taking things seriously.

However, meeting a Gemini dog often seems like meeting an old friend. It has a tail wag for anyone who takes the trouble to say hello and stroke it, and will always proffer a friendly paw to anyone who is feeling under the weather. The Gemini dog possesses powerful, healing vibrations that are very effective where there is any sort of infection.

GEMINI CAT

The Gemini cat possesses very sharp senses and is perhaps one of the most telepathic of creatures. It is usually very energetic with a strong sense of adventure. It has a cheeky mischievous side and the charisma to charm anyone and make them feel important.

Like the Gemini dog, the Gemini cat is extremely communicative and very loving. It possesses strong healing vibrations that are good for the treatment of almost any health condition.

CANCER DOG
ELEMENT WATER

As I mentioned at the beginning of this chapter both the Cancerian dog and cat are the most psychic of all the astrological signs. But, there can be an extremely negative side to the Cancerian dog, which can at times become very depressed, the result of an inherent emotional nature.

The Cancerian dog is a very 'needy' and emotional creature and has a great deal of love to give. In fact, it lives to love and be loved. Love is life's sustenance to a Cancerian dog and is more important to it than the very air it breathes. It may not be the most energetic of dogs physically, but mentally it has been everywhere and done everything.

The Cancerian dog can heal you with love alone. Its energies are very soothing and yet extremely vibrant and affect the human organism holistically.

CANCER CAT

Like the Cancerian dog, the Cancerian cat too is a dreamer, and one who is able to travel great distances without even moving from the comfort of the armchair. Its mind is never still, and if cats can be dreamers then the Cancerian cat is definitely that.

It possesses strong and incredibly vibrant healing vibrations, which can have a pronounced positive effect upon the human mind. This cat is very good to have around children when they are feeling unwell.

LEO DOG
ELEMENT FIRE

This creature possesses one of the strongest characters in the dog world and always likes to be the centre of attention. If dogs can be vain and arrogant then the Leo dog most certainly is. When it walks into a room it likes to be noticed, and if it is not then hide the cushions!

This canine is very strong and often exerts a great deal of power over its carers. It possesses the ability to influence the minds of its owners, and its energy can be extremely effective in the healing of headaches caused by tension, eyestrain or migraine. A cuddle from the Leo dog will relax you and take all your worries away.

LEO CAT

Just like the Leo dog, the Leo cat likes to be made a fuss of, and may therefore find it difficult to accept other creatures – especially dogs – in the family home. It can be extremely impatient and sometimes possesses a very volatile nature.

The Leo cat appears to have a soothing effect on the human mind, while at the same time an invigorating influence on the entire human organism. This creature will encourage the healing process of any dermatological condition, and will give strength to the nervous system.

VIRGO DOG
ELEMENT EARTH

The investigative powers of this creature may sometimes be miscon-strued as nosiness when, in fact, the Virgo dog simply likes to explore unknown territory and always welcomes a challenge. This quality is demonstrated by its 'sniffer' characteristics; its nose probably being its most sensitive organ, and its sense of smell extremely acute.

This is a fussy creature and may sometimes appear so snobby that it could well have been born into the canine aristocracy. It enjoys its home comforts but can sometimes be over-territorial in temperament.

Although possessing strong healing energies the Virgo dog lacks patience and can be quite temperamental to the extreme. It needs to feel happy and comfortable with someone before healing can take place. Nevertheless, its healing vibrations are extremely effective when mobility of the limbs is restricted. It also encourages recovery from illness by helping to raise the levels of vitality in the human organism.

VIRGO CAT

Like the Virgo dog, the Virgo cat has a sense of adventure and always welcomes a challenge. It is unpredictably moody and can appear unwell when in actual fact it is simply in a mood. This is a very resilient creature who will take anything thrown at it (within reason, that is).

The Virgo cat likes to be stroked and made a fuss of. It is nearly always a creature of strong habit and is usually very tidy almost to the point where it becomes depressed if things are in disarray. It possesses a very strong and sharp memory and can quickly attune itself to a family atmosphere. In saying that, the Virgo cat usually becomes known as his or her cat, and very rarely gives its affections to more than one person in the family.

The Virgo cat's healing vibrations extend over a broad spectrum of ailments, and this cat is always good to have around when you are feeling unwell, or simply under the weather.

LIBRA DOG
ELEMENT AIR

The dog born under the astrological sign of Libra is either very high or extremely low, emotionally speaking. There is very rarely a happy medium. However, warm, friendly and extremely persuasive, this dog can overwhelm its owner with affection, and is always mindful of its owner's state of health. Creatures born under the astrological sign of Libra are nearly always extremely attractive to look at. They possess an abundance of charisma with contagious personalities, never failing to light up a room. The Libra dog is the charmer of the canine world, loved by everyone for its pleasant disposition.

The Libra dog can release strong healing vibrations into the surrounding atmosphere, which are especially beneficial for sick and elderly people. It can calm an anxious person especially when cuddled (which it loves). The only faults of the Libra dog are its occasional outbursts of volatility and unpredictable mood swings, which very often limit its full healing potential.

LIBRA CAT

This creature is full of personality and character, and can literally charm the birds from the trees. It possesses stores of energy and vitality and is extremely invigorating to have around the home.

The Libra cat is extremely wise and always prefers to take charge and control over other creatures in the home. This cat's healing abilities are extremely effective where psychological and emotional illnesses are concerned and will also help to ease intense physical pain, particularly in the back.

SCORPIO DOG
ELEMENT WATER

The Scorpio dog is undoubtedly a force to be reckoned with! It is usually quiet and reserved with its feelings, but should you step out of line with it in some way, it will show you what it is really like below the serene surface. Yes, the Scorpio dog does not suffer fools gladly, and can be extremely volatile. It does not usually like to be cuddled too much and is a lover of its own company. This dog dislikes loud and boisterous people and due to its charismatic, yet understated charm, just being around a Scorpio dog is healing in itself.

Its healing energies have the effect of strengthening and precipitating a sick person's own energies, and also help to clear the mind. It can quite often be sufficient just to sit next to a Scorpio dog and stroke its fur gently a few times in order to receive its vibrant healing.

SCORPIO CAT

The Scorpio cat possesses many of the qualities possessed by the Scorpio dog. It is independent, quiet and occasionally standoffish. However, unlike the Scorpio dog, the cat simply cannot be still. It is forever on the move, both mentally and physically.

This creature's healing vibrations tend to have a very stabilising effect upon the human mind, promoting serenity and calmness within the nervous system. Its energies are quite cold and often feel like currents of static electricity when one strokes its fur.

SAGITTARIUS DOG
ELEMENT FIRE

Although an extremely lovable character, this creature can often be difficult to control. Its energies are all over the place making it extremely inconsistent. It has so many things to do and very little time in which to do them. It never seems to finish anything before it goes on to the next thing.

A spiritualised creature, the Sagittarius dog has a strong character and well-developed sense of humour. This dog gives a whole new meaning to animal individuality, and although it can be quite unpredictable, it can always be persuaded or encouraged with the use of the proverbial 'walkies'. Despite its erratic nature the Sagittarius dog is good to have around when one is feeling depressed or perhaps recovering from mental or emotional trauma.

SAGITTARIUS CAT

This creature has a sense of fun and certainly knows how to enjoy life. In fact, not only does it appear to live life to the full, but there never seems to be enough hours in the day for this cat to do all the things it wants to do. It loves to be loved and shown affection and its fun nature tends to draw people and other animals towards it.

The cat born under the astrological sign of Sagittarius discharges its healing energies in consistent waves. These have a remarkable effect upon most illnesses, particularly in the elderly.

CAPRICORN DOG
ELEMENT EARTH

This creature loves all the comforts of a secure and loving home life. Although a little laid back and quite stubborn, particularly in anxious moments, it never ruffles. This dog can be quite courageous and will often rush in where angels fear to tread.

These dogs are also extremely protective towards their owners, and do not welcome change at all. Moving home tends to make them feel somewhat moody and depressed, but being the resilient creatures they are, any negative emotions of self-pity and sadness are usually transient;however, the Capricorn dog quickly returns to its normal self. Its possessive and head strong nature can sometimes manifest as bossiness, and if it doesn't get its own way, it will throw a tantrum.

If dogs can be like 'old women' then the Capricorn dog is exactly that. Their natural instinct to mother their owners makes them magnificent healers and these dogs make wonderful P.A.T dogs for the elderly or mentally disabled. They are usually very protective where children are concerned, and as a result are extremely good canine healers. They are usually fairly evenly tempered; they like to be pampered and made a fuss of, and give their energies to anyone who needs help.

CAPRICORN CAT

This creature possesses all the qualities of the Capricorn dog and more. It has an inherent need to care for all other creatures, and can sometimes be too clingy where its owner is concerned. This creature is good to have around in times of sickness, and it will certainly not stray too far from an owner who is unwell. The owner of a Capricorn cat will benefit greatly from its vibrant healing energies, which can also have an incredible stimulating effect when there is a lack of energy.

AQUARIUS DOG
ELEMENT AIR

The dog born under the astrological sign of Aquarius nearly always possesses a pleasant and likeable disposition, and gives a whole new meaning to the saying 'Its bark is worst than its bite'. Although quite moody, it is a little pussycat really.

This creature appears to think a great deal, and as most certainly evolved a spiritual sensitivity and awareness. The one criticism is that the Aquarius dog does not always listen and may just carry on doing its own thing, regardless of what its owner wants. He is a natural healer, whose calming energies are effective on all manner of illnesses.

THE AQUARIUS CAT

This is perhaps one of the most charismatic pussycats on the planet and one who most probably has the power to convert a person who doesn't like animals to one who does. However, its playful nature can sometimes be misunderstood.

The cat born under the astrological sign of Aquarius will promote serenity and calmness in the human mind, and its warm fur will calm taut and anxious nerves.

PISCES DOG
ELEMENT WATER

The Pisces dog can often appear cold and unapproachable, but in reality it is warm, loving and extremely friendly. Its cautious and sensitive nature can sometimes make it appear insecure, and although it can take offence quite easily, it dislikes very few people. This dog's sensitivity and insecurity is typical of the majority of creatures born under a water sign, but here it necessitates an extremely loving home where it is treated as a part of the family.

This dog wants to heal everyone and make the whole world a better place to live in. It wants to be loved by everyone and expects everyone to want to stroke it. Its healing powers are quite extensive, but are particularly effective on those suffering with respiratory problems.

PISCES CAT

The Pisces cat is astute and very perspective. Its awareness of it surrounding environment is so sharp that you almost cut yourself on its fur! Although affectionate in nature, it can be very cautious and will only allow you to invade its space when it is absolutely certain of your intentions.

Piscean energies are extremely effective in encouraging the human organism to recover from illness. Its healing vibrations are very quick, and have the incredible effect of infusing a person with a surge of energy. This creature's fur is 'alive' with vitality, and just occasionally running one's fingers through it is indeed a tonic to the depleted and tired mind.

Although specific health conditions have been mentioned under each astrological sign, I feel it is important to point out that these are only suggestions and are in no way a substitute for conventional medicine. Although the healing powers of animals can be quite spontaneous, they should only be expected to complement conventional medical treatment and not to replace it.

Once the healing energy passes from your pet and is absorbed by your nervous system, the effects of it are usually holistic as the *whole* person benefits from the subtle energies, as opposed to merely the affected part of the body.

CHAPTER SIXTEEN

GROWING TO LOOK LIKE YOUR DOG

Although intended to be a serious study of the healing powers of animals, I thought at this point I would take a little detour and share with you some light-hearted observations I have made during the compiling of the material for this book.

The age old belief that we grow to look like our pets is not as silly as it sounds – it is in fact true!

To begin with, dogs are very much affected by their owners personality, and to some degree do make every effort to emulate, in their own way, their owner's characteristics and personality traits. Although this may not be obvious to an onlooker, once the dog has established itself in the family it begins to exhibit strong feelings of adulation and admiration for its master and carer. The creature starts to psychically and probably subconsciously mimic its owner's personality, or what it sees as its owner's personality. The dog somehow infiltrates its owner's personal energy field, gradually encouraging him or her to take on a subtle appearance of the dog itself. I know this will sound completely ridiculous even to some dog lovers, let alone those who do not like animals. Nonetheless, in my twenty years study I have come to conclude that this theory of dogs in particular is so true. The animal lover, however, cannot deny that their pet, to some greater or lesser degree, most definitely does influence them and really does exert an extremely strong control over what they do.

Our pets exert a far greater mental control over us than we realise, and they do influence us in ways we can't imagine. In fact, living in close proximity to the family pet brings about a psychic metamorphosis of the owner's personality, until eventually he or she appears not only to walk like their dog, but they may even subconsciously take on its stance and facial expressions. Furthermore, in my observations I have occasionally seen a man mimic his dog, from the walk to the wiggle – a mirror image almost of his canine friend. I'm not suggesting that everyone is affected in this way, but it does seem to occur in the majority of those who are devoted to their dog.

A dog of slender stature with an elongated face is often seen to be accompanied by a man or woman of slender stature with an elongated face. Whether or not this is mere coincidence is a point in question.

Nevertheless, this very strange and at times hilarious phenomenon is often to be seen in the park or in the street. It is not uncommon to see an overweight Bulldog, Rottweiler or Pit Bull terrier accompanied by an overweight owner. Sometimes, one only sees the similarities on second, closer inspection.

A slow and lazy dog is nearly always accompanied by a similar owner. Likewise, the boisterous, full of energy dog is often to be found with a lively, full of energy owner. I must say though that there are exceptions to this rule, as some dogs possess far too much energy for their owners, who may be seen lagging tiredly behind their sprinting canine.

Cat owners do not escape the psychology of this phenomenon. The endearing qualities often seen in the family cat are nearly always mirrored in the human who is thought to be closest to it.

However, cats do not affect their owner's appearance in the same way as dogs do, but most certainly mentally encourage changes in their human's personality and temperament. Like cats themselves, cat owners often fall into two categories: the one who remains calm and collected, even when in the midst of panic and chaos; and the worried, anxious, nervy one who lives perpetually on their nerves, and is always under a veritable cloud of worry and stress.

Nevertheless, I have known some cat owners to almost take

on the look of their cat. Beverly Nicholls, a well-known writer and lover of cats, now deceased, had, to my mind, an almost cat-like appearance. He obviously had an affinity with cats and wrote some extremely interesting pieces about them.

There are, of course, some limitations. I am not suggesting that the keeper of ferrets will come to look like the lithe creatures he or she keeps, or that the lizard fanatic will take on a reptilian nature – although there is always that possibility. Simply, that in the same way humans assimilate the behaviour of the circle of friends they spend their time with and look towards for advice and love, so they will emulate the pet they adore as much as a child of their own. Of course, this is done at a subconscious level, and the owners of pets are unaware that they are actually doing it.

OUR PETS INFLUENCE US

Cats and dogs have played an extremely important part in the life of the human species. Dogs have always worked with and lived alongside man, and have evolved mentally and spiritually as a direct consequence. I am quite certain that our dogs and cats are fully aware of the power they hold over humans, and I am convinced that they exploit this to the full. Our pets, in their own beneficial way, are extremely manipulative, and far wiser and more intelligent than we give them credit for. It makes sense then, that if our pets have such a strong and powerful influence over our minds and psychic natures, then they have the ability to make us better when we are ill.

It is my belief, and a belief that is shared by an increasing number of people, that animals possess such metaphysical powers as were once possessed and used by our primitive forebears. Although we have forgotten exactly how to use these powers, the Animal Kingdom has not. Because of the interactive natures of cats and dogs, these powers are somehow transmuted into potent healing forces that are able to affect the human organism in an extremely positive way. So, simply having animals around is very good for the psychological fitness of the human mind, and also for the health of the human body.

Whilst most dogs are territorial by nature, they are much more so where their owners are concerned, and literally weave a psychic veil over their human companions, in an effort to control and repel other animals. This does not always work as people who have a strong liking for animals emit a powerful subtle scent that informs other creatures that this human is an animal lover. While the person who does not relate to any animal other than their own pet dog will often find that other dogs will either avoid them completely, or perhaps show aggression towards them.

Although most dogs, with the exception of a few, are quite tolerant of humans, they are extremely choosy, and are often very good judges of character. So, when a dog's *will* has been broken down through consistent acts of cruelty towards it, not only does it take a great deal of time and patience to rebuild its confidence in humans, but a lot of time needs to be spent healing the creature spiritually. When a dog has been cruelly treated its eyes reflect a deep disappointment that only love from a new owner can heal.

There is no doubt about it – cats and dogs are characters, and the more one gets to know one's dog, the more this becomes a reality. Those who love cats and dogs tend to treat them like children, scolding them when they misbehave, cuddling them when they have been hurt, talking to them and laughing at them when they are in a playful mood. Our pets make us what they want us to be. They bring out in us those qualities that often lie deeply buried in our emotions.

ANIMALS TRULY HAVE THE POWER TO HEAL SIMPLY BY LOVING US.

CHAPTER SEVENTEEN

MAN'S CRUELTY TO ANIMALS

Cruelty to animals is an abomination and something which deserves punishment far greater than is witnessed today in a court of law. The souls of those who slaughter animals either for fun or for the sake of it are lacking in the very fabric that makes us human beings. As an animal lover I just can't understand what makes some people delight in killing or maiming animals. It's completely alien to me, and the very thought of it makes me feel sick and very sad.

We most certainly need animals far more than we know. Few of us recognise the pivotal role animals play in the evolution of man's emotions. In fact, their very presence on this planet alone creates a healing atmosphere that is vitally important to the spiritual equilibrium of humanity, and I am quite certain that we could not exist in a world devoid of animals.

The dawn chorus and the movement of wings against the air are integrated parts of some mystical symphony composed by nature, which is so essential for the continuity of life. We should therefore feel privileged to share this planet with the Animal Kingdom, and it is time to realise that our need for them is far greater than we are presently able to understand.

However, there are some people in this world who are not just content to dislike animals, but they actually delight in subjecting them to the most appalling cruelty, without experiencing a hint of shame, guilt or conscience. These individuals often look upon animals as creatures without souls, or simply disease carriers possessing no feelings or awareness.

Cruelty to animals is by no means restricted to cats and dogs. On the contrary, the whole of the Animal Kingdom is affected in one way or another, from the cruel hunting of the fox, (now banned in the UK), to the senseless slaughter of the noble elephant in Africa for their ivory tusks.

In recent years we have seen the horrific torture of the bear in China. Kept alive in the most hideous conditions, its bile is extracted regularly and painfully from its gut, simply to provide a so-called 'miracle cure' – mainly for consumption in the Western world.

Whilst most people could not withstand either the stench and horror of an abattoir, or the sight of those defenceless and terrified creatures being led to their slaughter, those same people can, however, tuck into a succulent steak, or tear the flesh from a breast of chicken. The fact that they are eating the corpse of a living creature is nearly always conveniently ignored.

Humans are conditioned from childhood to believe that eating the flesh of animals is acceptable. To salve our consciences further we refer to the Bible, in which we can read how the flesh of the fatted calf was consumed. Eating meat must be alright then, we tell ourselves, as it is mentioned in the Bible. Anyway, as long as someone else does the slaughtering, and we do not have to see any blood flowing, or hear the screams of terror, or see any heaps of still, warm corpses, then consuming the cooked product on our plates is fine.

After all, why should meat-eating be any more acceptable than consuming human flesh? For animals are animated by the same force that animates the human form, and they are in fact a lot closer to God, and far more reliable than we humans.

Although meat-eating has always been a part of our culture, at least in the Western world, attitudes are certainly now beginning to change towards the habit. Science informs us that meat in our diet is no longer vitally important for a healthy body.

Dogs, rats, mice, monkeys, rabbits and many more defenceless animals are being subjected to laboratory experiments in the name of science: do the creatures themselves possess a voice that protests? Or is their wellbeing reliant on those dedicated and courageous people who speak out for them, and continually proclaim that 'Animals do have rights'?

Yes: there is most certainly a voice that speaks, and this voice is collectively made up of every single animal on this planet, creating a force which is far greater and more powerful than any exhibited by man.

Each and every animal on this planet is linked one to the other, in a mystical network within which a powerful force is created and passed around. Even the family dog, secure in the love of the family, is not ignorant of the plight and torment of its brother animals in far off places, for he too is an integral part of this great animal network.

But what of those who inflict so much misery and suffering on animals, and whose cruel acts often evade the punishment of the law? Is justice ever brought about?

By inflicting suffering of any kind upon an innocent creature, one might as well inflict suffering upon oneself. The Animal Kingdom as a whole is the very foundation upon which the evolution of man's emotional nature has its true being.

Cruelty to animals never passes unrecognised as the perpetrators of such cruelty take upon themselves great spiritual burdens. Consequently, the pain they inflict upon an innocent creature is eventually returned to them two-fold, if not in this life, then most certainly in the next.

But apart from man's wilful malice towards animals, we should not forget the thoughtless and careless destruction of animals in our countryside and on our roads. The wild bird population is decreasing enormously in numbers as more and more birds are seen lying dead on the country roads. Unaware of the danger, millions of hedgehogs are dying beneath the wheels of cars because of man's haste and lack of care. Badgers are baited, rabbits are either shot or killed on the roads, pheasants and grouse are allowed to grow fat until the season when they can 'lawfully' be shot.

Cruelty to animals varies from culture to culture, and surely represents the degree of spirituality attained therein. A great deal of cruelty exhibited towards the Animal Kingdom appears to have 'entertainment' value, which makes it more acceptable to the people of that particular country. Bull fighting is a prime example – a hideous and extremely cruel 'sport' in which no mercy is shown to that magnificent creature, which is tormented and tortured before its almost ritualistic slaying.

In the same country donkeys are thrown from the tops of buildings during certain festive occasions. If the creature is lucky it will die immediately, if not it will suffer a slow, agonising death. It has been said that it is only the uneducated of the country that participates in such barbaric events. I am quite certain that this is no excuse for sheer cruelty!

It would appear that because animals cannot speak with words that we understand, they are often regarded as mindless, soul-less creatures, without feelings, hopes or dreams.

The entire Animal Kingdom is being exploited, and is slowly diminishing in size, but still these innocent creatures continue to provide us with so much enjoyment. Their very presence on this planet creates a subtle atmosphere essential to the human soul. We simply could not live on a planet devoid of animals, for, along with the food we eat, the water we drink, and the air we breathe, animals are indeed an essential part of human life.

But today a new epoch is beginning to dawn, as a wave of compassion, understanding and respect for nature and the Animal Kingdom dawns upon man's collective consciousness. Although this 'new' awareness will pass by, sadly unheeded by the majority of our planet's human residents, that minority whose consciousness has already, or is now in the process of unfolding, will find themselves moving closer to a spiritual awakening, of which animals are an integral part.

Throughout the ages many great writers, philosophers and

orators have put into words their own deepest feelings regarding animals and man's treatment of them. I have listed some of their quotations here, many of which I am sure you will find quite moving.

WHAT FAMOUS PEOPLE HAVE TO SAY ABOUT ANIMALS

Stroke not the animal with one hand and pick its bones with the other.
TEACHINGS OF TALL PINE 1975

Animals share with us the privilege of having a soul.
PYTHAGORAS, B.C. 551.

What have the oxen done, those faithful guileless beasts, harmless and simple, born to a life of toil?
OVID, B.C. 43.

On seeing a dog being beaten, pitying he said, 'Stop and beat it not, for the soul is that of a friend'.
XENOPHANES B.C. 545.

Hurt not animals.
TRIPTOLEMUS, A.D. 50

A righteous man regardeth the life of his beast.
OLD TESTAMENT PROVERBS X11,10.

Two by two the animals entered the Ark, as God commanded Noah.
GENESIS, CH. 6, V.19-20.

And God said, 'For every beast of the forest is mine, and the cattle upon a thousand hills. I know all the fowls of the mountains, and the wild beasts are mine'.
PSALM 50, V. 9-11

The wolf shall dwell with the lamb, the leopard shall lie down with the kid…and a little child shall lead them.
ISAIAH, CH. X1, V.8

No beast is there on earth or fowl that flieth, nothing have we passed over in the book of Eternal Decrees, that shall not be gathered unto the Lord.
KORAN.

There is not an animal on earth, nor a flying creature on two wings, but they are people like unto you.
KORAN.

A fleet horse or greyhound do not make a noise when they have done well…neither should man.
MARCUS AURELUS.

Even savage animals, if kept confined, forget their natural courage.
TACITUS.

For every creature shall be delivered from the bondage of corruption into the glorious liberty of men.
For we know that every creature groaneth with us and travaileth in pain even unto his time.
ROMANS, CH. 8, V. 21-22.

God created humans and animals for their mutual benefit.
T. COSLMEILLE OF IONA.

Animals have rights in themselves because of their capacity to feel both pain and pleasure.
ST CIARAN OF OSSORY.

Who loves me will love my dog also.
ST BERNARD.

Who loves me loves my dog.
LE ROUX DE LINEY, 13th CENTURY. MS.

I could descant in all candour on the glories of the worm.
ST AUGUSTINE.

The pious duty of children is to feed their parents, and dogs and horses must also receive their food.
CONFUCIUS.

All things are born of the Unborn, and from this unity of life flows brotherhood and compassion for all creatures.
BUDDHA.

Postpone the entrance of Nirvana until each blade of grass has entered into Enlightenment.
IBID.

In Buddhism we are told that animals possessed of the Buddha nature are in time destined for Heaven.
CHRISTMAS HUMPHRIES.

The great lovers of men have also been great lovers of animals. St Francis of Assis and his wolf, St Hugh of Lincoln and his swan, St Jerome his lion, St Peter the cock, St Benedict the raven, St John the Evangelist, his red-legged partridge.
REV. W.H. BARNARD

The lamb, the pelican and the unicorn are the symbols of Christ.
BREWER.

He entered into Jerusalem on a colt, whereon yet no man had sat.
ST LUKE, CH. 19, V. 30.

*The behaviour of men to the lower animals, and their behaviour to each
    other, bears constant relationship.*
HERBERT SPENCER.

Have a care for a silent dog, and still water.
LATIN PROVERB.

Thou wast not born for death, immortal bird!
KEATS

God made all creatures, and gave them our love and our fear,
To give sign, we and they are his children, one family here.
ROBERT BROWNING.

A horse misused upon the road, calls to heaven for human blood.
WILLIAM BLAKE.

*In life, the dog the firmest friend, the first to welcome, foremost to
    defend.*
BYRON

*Let none count themselves wise who have not in imagination felt the
    pain of the vivisected.*
JOHN COWPER POWYS.

Animals do not lie awake weeping for their sins,
They do not discuss their duty to God,
Have no mania for owning things,
Kneel to no one of their kind...
WALT WHITMAN

Animals have these advantages – no theologians to instruct them, no
    funeral costs, and no lawsuits over wills.
VOLTAIRE

The best thing about man is his dog.
IBID.

It often happens that a man is more humanely related to a dog or cat
    than to any human being.
HENRY D THOREAU.

The more I see of men, the more I like dogs.
MADAM DE STAEL.

No flocks that range the valley free, to slaughter I condemn. Taught by
    that power that pities me, I learn to pity them.
GOLDSMITH-VICAR OF WAKEFIELD.

Man is mad: he cannot make a flea, and yet he will make gods by the
    dozens.
MONTAIGNE.

He prayeth well, who loveth well both man and bird and beast.
SAMUEL TAYLOR COLERIDGE.

The animal world is a manifestation of God's power, and demands
    respect and consideration. The desire to kill animals, unnecessary
    harshness and callous cruelty towards them, must always be
    condemned.
POPE PIUS THE TWELFTH.

A mouse is a miracle enough to stagger six trillions of infidels.
EDWARD NAYLOR.

...Medicine with cruel heartlessness has tortured sensitive animals in reckless scientific investigation with no direct or indirect relation to human good.
BISHOP PHILLIP BROOKS.

The greatness of a nation and their moral progress can be judged by the way their animals are treated.
GANDHI.

If we have spirits that persist, animals have, if we know after death who we are, they do.
JOHN GALSWORTHY

Animals are such agreeable friends, they ask no questions, they pass no criticisms.
GEORGE ELIOT

Kittens have a very inconvenient habit. Whatever you say to them they always purr.
LEWIS CARROLL.

Dogs laugh, but they laugh with their tails.
MAX EASTMAN.

Saith the Lord, 'I come in little things. The glancing wings of eager birds, the softly pattering feet of furred and gentle beats.
EVELYN UNDERHILL.

Men who spend their days inflicting atrocious cruelties on helpless living creatures, must turn them into something like cruel devils.
BISHOP BAGSHAW.

In studying the traits and dispositions of the so-called lower animals, and contrasting them with man's, I find the result humiliating to me.

MARK TWAIN.

Man is the only animal that blushes, or needs to.

IBID.

Animal 'sportsmen' give living creatures pain in order to get pleasure themselves. One should derive pleasure from relieving other creatures' pain.

PROF. CHRISTOPHER EVANS, THEOLOGIAN.

Oxford is still beautiful, in spite of the screaming of the rabbits in the home of the vivisector.

OSCAR WILDE AFTER A VISIT TO OXFORD.

The evil practice of vivisection is damnable on its effect on human character.

JOHN CHANDLER WHITE
EPISCOPAL BISHOP OF SPRINGFIELD ILLINOIS.

Vivisection makes medical students less tender of suffering, begets indifference to it, and deadens their humanity.

DR. HENRY J. BIGELOW,
PROFESSOR OF SURGERY, HARVARD MEDICAL SCHOOL.

The dog is man's best friend.

OGDEN NASH.

Wild animals never kill for sport. Man is the only one to whom the torture and death of his fellow creatures is amusing in itself.

J.A FROYDE

I'd like to know what basis of morality and who gives us the moral right to take the life of any living thing.
SPIKE MILLIGAN.

The one absolutely unselfish friend that man can have in this selfish world is his dog.
SENATOR GEORGE GRAHAM WEST.

Vivisection is a mistaken scientific approach to the problem of human health.
VICTOR REINAECKER, F.PH. S

Extreme horror of cruelty is the mark of the spiritual man.
G.B. SHAW.

CHAPTER EIGHTEEN

THE WRONG PROGRAMME

For humans the possibility that we survive bodily death has always held a great fascination. The very idea that we might be given the opportunity to be reborn once again into the physical world, for a continued existence, is even more exciting.

Although the concept of rebirth does not appear in modern day Christian philosophy it did form an integral part of early Christian teachings, but for some reason was removed in order to modernise Christianity. Christianity though is quite specific about its ideas of the survival of the human soul, and these ideas exclude animals completely, even though the Animal Kingdom has played such an important role in the work of numerous saints throughout the ages. The Church has always cloaked the after-death experience in mystery, and made any knowledge of it accessible only through its priests and ministers.

As animals have always been looked upon as the lesser, although innocent creatures in the scheme of things, the chance of them being re-born into another corporeal life, let alone surviving the physical death, seems to many unthinkable. After all, if this concept were accepted, where would it leave the animals whose flesh has been consumed by humans from time immemorial? To complicate the whole issue even more, the concept of rebirth is not as straightforward as one might imagine, or at least not where animals are concerned.

Whereas many believe that humans make a definite and clear choice about subjecting themselves to re-embodiment, animals are not given the opportunity to make that decision. They are therefore drawn into the great wheel of rebirth in accordance with their evolutionary status, and pulled along in the endless cycle of rebirth.

However, the incredible intelligence of some domestic animals makes it quite apparent that there is something other than animal instinct in operation, and that some creatures are most certainly nearing the end of their great journey of perpetual rebirth.

As with humans, animals too are born into a particular programme. The human soul has a specific mission when it is incarnated into a physical body, and has to fulfil certain spiritual requirements. Eradicating habits, and developing those qualities that are absent, certainly do form an integral part of this mission, but for the animal soul the Great Cycle of Rebirth is a necessity and cannot be avoided.

Through this process the animal develops tolerance, sensitivity and an understanding of man. The lives of some animals often appear to be no more than a punishment for them, and yet this life often produces animals with the gentlest of natures.

Looking into the eyes of some animals one often sees a wise creature staring out as though saying 'What am I doing here in this body? Please help me. I should not be here.'

For some reason during the great mysterious process of rebirth, things can go wrong as the soul begins its vibratory descent through the manifested worlds of the cosmos to eventually become encased in a physical body. Its attainments and previous memories maybe allowed to filter through into the creature's consciousness, when in fact all this data should be stored, and inaccessible to the incarnated soul. This causes the animal to be extremely sensitive and to be in the possession of an almost human-like intelligence. These creatures possess a deep understanding of humans, and nearly always exhibit qualities that set them apart from other animals.

A whole group of animals can find themselves caught up in 'The Wrong Programme' so to speak, when the process of reincarnation takes place. When affected collectively the individual animals may experience extremely difficult and at worst unhappy lives. They may be born into an environment of cruelty and deprivation, and be subjected to the most difficult and sad existence.

Because the pitiful creature has been so unfortunate as to incarnate into the wrong programme, its life is but a short sojourn in comparison to what might have been had the process gone according to plan. Such unfortunate creatures experience a brief rest after death, before then being drawn back into the Great Wheel of Rebirth.

On their return to the physical world they prove to be a huge presence, possessing an incredible intelligence and persona. Such animals possess amazing psychic abilities, and their very presence in a family creates a wonderful healing balm that cannot fail to affect all who come into contact with it.

Although these sorts of family pets are often extremely difficult to define, when in their presence one often has the strong feelings of standing before a creature greater than the average domesticated pet. They very often appear extremely wise and exude personality and character. This furry creature enjoys human company and loves to be touched. It interacts perfectly well with humans, takes extreme care with children and disabled people, and knows exactly when its owner is unhappy or unwell. They very quickly establish themselves as the 'head' of the household and the most important member in the family. In fact, these little creatures are not only huge characters with magnificent senses of humour, but their charm also enables them to win over the coldest of hearts.

In my quest for material for this book I learned of a man who had spent most of his adult life in and out of prison for committing crimes of violence. He was a persistent offender whose life was in chaos. He was lonely and very unhappy, causing him to drink more than he should, and this indulgence only contributed even more to his aggression and violence.

Life for Kenny changed dramatically when he rescued a young mongrel that was being savaged by two Alsatians in the park. Both Kenny and Little Totty (as Kenny named the dog) escaped with only a few cuts and bruises, but Kenny's heart had been won almost immediately.

This special tiny mongrel and he became very close friends. Within weeks Kenny's drinking had practically stopped. He became more relaxed and much more pleasant to be around. Little Totty seemed to take all the aggression and anger away from him, and Kenny suddenly developed a completely different attitude towards everything and everyone. There was no doubt about it – Kenny became a different person altogether.

This all happened in 2003, and Kenny is now in regular employment, and has not been in trouble with the police since Totty came into his life. In fact, he is now making plans to marry his girlfriend of two years. Kenny happily admits that the credit for all this goes to Little Totty, his little mongrel friend. Kenny proudly tells anyone who will listen to him that the little dog has healed and transformed his life completely.

I recall as a child a stray dog running into our house on a cold foggy January night. Jack, as we affectionately called him, stayed with us as our guest for three years, winning his cheeky way into all our hearts.

Being myself a somewhat sickly child, often at home ill, Jack became my constant companion and friend. He slept beside me, played with me and protected me.

Then, one similar cold, foggy night, as though he was called away by some sacred mysterious voice, Jack ran off into the fog, never to be seen again, taking with him a huge piece of our hearts. Jack had most certainly been born into the wrong programme, and frequently appeared to be lost in thought, his large brown eyes always anxiously searching around him.

A person who dislikes animals would probably dismiss the whole idea of this book as sentimental mush. But this just proves my point, doesn't it? Only animal lovers can be privy to such a concept, and only they would truly understand what I am saying that, *'Not All Angels Have Wings.'*

CHAPTER NINETEEN

LEARN TO SPEAK TO AND UNDERSTAND YOUR PET

Are you aware that you can learn to speak to your pet and understand everything it is trying to say? I'm quite certain that most people will dismiss this suggestion as being quite ridiculous, and those who don't will probably affirm that their dog or cat understands every word they say to it, and vice versa. The truth is though, the closer the relationship you have with your pet, the stronger and more profound your communications with it will be. After all, our pets understand us, so why can't we take the trouble to understand them?

There are many things about your pet's true character that you are unable to see. Most people tend to take their pets for granted, and often wrongly assume – simply because they use a completely different system of communication – that their cat or dog cannot 'speak'. The frequency of an animal's mind is much higher than ours and, being unencumbered by those things that cause us so much stress and anxiety, there is far greater clarity in the reception and transmission of their thought processes. So by carefully attuning your mind to your pet's vibrations you can learn to talk to it and understand what it is trying to say to you.

By the shifting of your consciousness until the correct frequency has been acquired, using a simple technique I have called 'thought transmutation', you will be able to understand that universal language of thought, enabling you to then break down the subtle barrier that separates the human mind from that of the animal's. There is certainly nothing complicated in the process, and I'm quite sure that you will find it quite enjoyable. All you need to do is to pick the right moment to relax with your pet, when you are both in a quiet and relaxed state of mind.

If you are very close to your dog or cat you will probably understand every mood and facial expression. You will know when it wants to go for its obligatory walk, and you will know exactly when it is not feeling too well. In other words, you have become accustomed to having your pet around the home, and its presence will most probably be felt in every room. A family pet is usually a huge presence in the home, and so whenever it is not there, for whatever reason, its absence is most certainly felt. Such a close relationship suggests that the connection you have with your pet transcends mere physical contact.

STAGE ONE:

- *Sit comfortably beside your pet, either on the floor or on the sofa.*
- *With your eyes closed simply stroke your pet gently, feeling the warmth of its fur between your fingertips.*
- *At the same time mentally reassure it of your love for it. Allow your thoughts to be processed into pictures, and then make every effort to transmit those pictures to your pet. In fact, spend some time on the transmission of your thoughts, occasionally opening your eyes to check your pet's response.*
- *Feel a deep spiritual bond with your pet, and be conscious of its love and devotion for you. It is important that you use all your senses as you mentally process the feelings your pet is transmitting to you.*
- *Become totally relaxed, allowing your breathing to be nice and rhythmical, slow and deep.*
- *At this point you should notice a marked change in the way your pet is breathing. In fact, it should be noticeably slower and more evenly spaced.*
- *Now, in your mind's eye, try to see your pet leading you through an archway of intense golden light. Watch yourself following it, and emerge into a spacious hall with a glass-domed ceiling.*
- *Mentally look up at the glass dome, and see that it is translucent,*

like mother of pearly. Make every effort to maintain the imagery, resisting all temptation at this point to open your eyes.

- *Occasionally run your fingers through your pet's fur, again feeling its warmth and reassuring energies.*
- *Mentally see the wall around the hall shimmering with many different colours and smell a sweet fragrance in the air.*
- *Bright light cascades down from the domed ceiling, breaking up into a myriad of colours as it falls into the centre of the hall, forming a pool of sparkling light there.*
- *Follow your pet to this point in the centre of the hall and allow yourself to be bathed in the different colours. For a brief moment become aware of your pet lying with you on the settee, and then immediately return to the imagery.*
- *Feel that intense closeness and oneness with your pet, and feel as though you are floating on a coloured cloud together. Hold onto your pet, and again feel its warmth and love.*
- *Now allow yourself to mentally move across the spacious hall towards the far side.*
- *Having reached the wall see yourself and your pet passing through it, as if by magic, and find yourself and your pet back in your living room, both feeling totally relaxed and serene.*
- *Open your eyes and take a look at your pet. He or she may be looking at you and wondering about the whole exercise, or may have drifted into an even deeper sleep.*

The first part of the exercise is to allow your mind to blend with your pet. In the initial stages of the exercise your pet will simply have experienced a series of images passing through its mind. You, however, will have established a very significant psychological 'connection' with your pet, in preparation for the next part of the exercise. Incidentally, the various stages of the programme can be followed at different times and not necessarily all in one go. Besides, it's highly unlikely that your pet will remain alongside of you for the duration of the whole programme.

STAGE TWO

- *Sit quietly next to your pet, and before you touch it breathe rhythmically for a few moments with your eyes closed. This ensures that your mind is quiet and you are totally relaxed.*
- *Place one hand gently on the top of your pet's head, ensuring that you are only touching it very lightly.*
- *Begin stroking its head and neck slowly, with your fingertips gently caressing your pet's fur.*
- *When you feel as though 'something' is passing from you to your pet, establish this extremely important connection by sending it some simple mental commands, such as 'If you can hear me, stretch your body,' or perhaps 'Lick my hand.'*
- *At first there may be no positive response from your pet as it may simply not be listening to you. Some animals have an extremely short attention span, so this phase of the experiment might require quite a lot of patience on your part. However, if you are determined to achieve the desired results, you will need to persevere..*
- *It may be, though, that your pet responds immediately. This will depend on whether or not your pet is in 'receive mode.'*
- *Once you have received a response a further mental command should be given – one which requires some physical effort from your pet.*
- *This time try 'Go to your bowl and have a drink of water' for example. Send this command no more than three times, and then pause for five minutes before sending it again.*
- *Should there still be no response, leave it for a short while longer before trying it again.*
- *Take time with the experiment, and even if it takes a couple of weeks try to persevere with it. If you have a close, loving relationship with your pet it will eventually work.*
- *If you are really serious about the exercise it may also be a good idea to keep a record of your results, so that you can assess your progress. This may perhaps help you to see which approach*

would be the best and most effective. Because you know your pet well, it might also be necessary to modify the experiment a little, either to make it easier for your little friend, or even to make it more difficult.

When you are absolutely certain that the results achieved represent your pet's positive responses to your mental commands, the next step is to listen to what it is saying to you.

This exercise is an ideal way to cultivate a telepathic relationship with your pet, thereby opening a whole new mode of communication, so that you will then able to have mental conversations with your little friend. Working on the premise that this process of thought transference is possible, as dogs and cats think in pictures, then it should also apply to the thoughts of your pet and the conversations you have with it.

As one would imagine the thinking process of an animal is completely different to ours. I doubt very much that they mentally contemplate the mysteries of the universe, or even try to work out some complicated mathematical equation. However, one can rest assured that animals certainly do *think*. The minds of both cats and dogs are very much like radar, and are often continually scanning their surroundings. Animals also possess the ability to recall events that have been significant or important in some way to them – and not only simple instructions which have been repeated several times. We only assume that we have to speak out loud to enable our pets to hear us. Apparently this is not so. As previously stated, dogs and cats think in pictures and are able to 'pick-up' our thoughts very easily. The problem is the majority of us only try this for so long before losing interest. You've got to *know* that it works and persevere. Should you not be convinced that the process of thought transference actually works, then it won't!

Once a dog or cat forms a deep emotional relationship with a human, that person becomes the main focus of the creature's life.

Although dogs demonstrate this emotional attachment more openly than cats, a cat still has this mental and emotional bond nonetheless, but tends to be more philosophical about it – more laid back even.

STAGE THREE

- *Once rapport has been established between owner and pet, and the previous experimental processes have been practised regularly – and with some degree of success – spend some time relaxing with your pet in a nice quiet spot.*
- *As we have already established cats and dogs think in pictures, and these pictures once transmitted are sometimes converted automatically into definite thoughts.*
- *Speak to your pet mentally, making sure that you speak very slowly. Although the thought processes of animals are believed to be of a much higher frequency than those transmitted by the human mind, when our pet is receiving our thoughts it needs time to focus and to comprehend.*
- *So, when you transmit a question to your pet, do it several times and then pause for a minute. Then, repeat the question only this time converting it into pictures where possible.*
- *You may in fact find it easier to go through the whole process using pictures.*
- *Before you begin you may in fact need time to consider how exactly you can use pictures to transmit to your pet in this way.*
- *When you have decided which pictures you are going to use, ensure that you have condensed the question into as few pictures as possible, and then begin the transmission to your pet in a rhythmical and consistent way.*
- *Although your pet is far from stupid, you have to understand that it is not used to you using this mode of communication, and so he or she will need a little time to mentally absorb the process you are using to transmit your thoughts to it.*
- *If you are asking your dog to go and retrieve something from the*

next room, one of its toys for example, make certain that you take every effort to create one picture as opposed to a sequence of pictures to convey your command, as the latter would only confuse your pet.

- *A simple question such as 'Are you happy?' should receive an immediate simple response, such as a lick, a wag of the tail, or even just a raised head to look at you. Always include your pet's name in the question. For example, 'Are you happy, George?'*
- *With a question such as this transmitting your feeling will suffice, as opposed to pictures. The most common response to this question is often more a physical one, such as the lick, a raised paw, rather than a thought.*

Just spending time close to your pet, enjoying its wonderful healing vibrations, and listening to the vibratory motion of its body, will enable you very quickly to become attuned to its mind, and to understand the language it is speaking. Developing this ability to speak to your pet also enables you to know when it is unwell, or perhaps feeling sad for some reason. Once it realises that you are making an effort to communicate with it, your pet will endeavour to help you all it can.

People who work seriously with animals, and who are dedicated to their work – vets, or those who work in animal shelters – often, without even realising it, become so attuned to animals that they seem to know exactly what they are thinking or even how they are feeling.

It is not as difficult as one might imagine to understand the language of animals. If you have a close relationship with your pet you are halfway to understanding what exactly it is saying to you. Look upon it as merely speaking a different language, but one that you can most certainly learn.

Another interesting point is that animals are either attracted to, or repelled by, certain colours. You may notice, for instance, that your cat likes to curl up on the table when there is a blue tablecloth draped over it. Or perhaps it enjoys sleeping on the chair with pink covers, or by the window with the yellow glass.

If you have noticed your pet's preferences for certain colours, it might just be more sensitive to colour vibrations than you think. Should this be the case I would suggest that you exploit the use of colour when your pet is not very well.

CHAPTER TWENTY

COLOUR POWER, YOUR PET AND YOUR HOME

As previously mentioned dogs and cats are extremely sensitive to colour, and as I have said in a previous chapter surrounding it with specific shades and tones of colour can often calm down a boisterous creature, or even revitalise one lacking in energy. However, much more than this can be achieved by combining the powerful energies of colour with your pet's own healing forces.

Moving into a new house is stressful enough, but moving to a house with an unpleasant atmosphere will not only create a lot of unhappiness and depression for the family who have moved there, but at worst it can cause everyone's health to deteriorate, and may even have broader implications in the long term. A well-balanced metaphysical atmosphere of a home is of paramount importance to the health and well being of the family. However, the first member of the household to 'feel' an oppressive environment will always be the family pet, who can quickly fall into a depression, lose its appetite and ultimately have no energy. An unlucky house may not have anything to do with the present occupants, but may simply be the result of a build up of negative energy created by the thoughts and emotions of all those who have lived there previously. The very suggestion of this to a sceptic would most probably be dismissed as quite ridiculous, but this is a recognised Quantum scientific fact and one which is today widely accepted in scientific as well as metaphysical circles. A negative atmosphere can adversely affect the health of the whole family, physically as well as psychologically.

A house that is charged with negative psychic energy is often like a time bomb waiting to go off, or even like a volcano on the point of eruption. The more unpleasant feelings it creates, the more powerful it becomes, as the minds of its occupants perpetuate this energy even more with feelings of despondency, sadness and depression. And so it goes on. Although the examples I have listed are in the extreme, any atmosphere can be transformed using simple colour healing methods.

In fact, it matters very little how long the family have lived in the house, and they may have always been unhappy there, but the time bomb can explode at any moment, or the volcano erupt, releasing the dormant negative energies into action. We all know only too well how we can be affected by an oppressive atmosphere, and how a miserable one can overwhelm us when we walk into it for the first time. A miserable atmosphere is quite contagious and it is able to spread very quickly.

No sooner are the emotions of people released into the atmosphere when they are impregnated into the subtle nature of the bricks and mortar of the building itself, infusing it with power and vitality, and gradually making the house come 'alive' with a living personality all of its own. The subtle character that has been created in the house in fact represents all the minds of the people who have lived there throughout the years, and who have, in their own way, contributed to the present atmosphere. The metaphysical nature of a house with a heavy and oppressive atmosphere consists of pockets of subtle energy, capable of affecting each member of the family in different ways.

Although there are many ways in which the subtle atmosphere of a house may be cleared, it usually suffices simply to have a pet around the home. Because of a dog and cat's sensitivity to the environment and to the vibrations of colour, our pets can be used as vehicles for the transmutation of positive energy, clearing the negative energy and transforming the atmosphere completely.

We must first of all try to understand that collectively the colour arrangement of the decor of the house represents the way the house is psychically polarised, and dismal colours will influence all those who live there in the same way. Apart from this, dark and dismal colours in the decor tend to retain negative emotions, whilst light and brighter colours repell the same.

Therefore, the subtle vibrations of the colour scheme of the house, that may already be producing some negative energy to begin with, may also have a profound effect upon the health of any pets you might have. This might sound somewhat bizarre to anyone who is not familiar with the phenomenon of colour vibrations, but it is a scientific concept that has been used for thousands of years, particularly in ancient Egypt.

For the purpose of 'cleansing' and creating a healing atmosphere, it certainly helps the process to encourage as much light into the room as possible. Perhaps a few mirrors strategically situated will help to create the desired illusion of brightness. This most certainly helps when there has been quite a lot of sickness in the home. Light created by the illusion of mirrors helps greatly to eliminate the negative vibrations of illness, thus facilitating the cleansing process more effectively

Allow your pet to be present during the colour transformation. Take an occasional break to stroke and play with it, allowing some interaction to take place.

Remember to experiment as much as possible, using as many different colours as you can, and allowing your personal tastes to take a break.

It is certainly a good idea to create a separate area in the house for your dog, especially as he is one of the family, and most probably the most important one in the house.

Although dogs enjoy interacting in family life, it is also advisable to allow them their own space if possible, where they can be alone with their thoughts, toys and other playthings.

Pale blues and different shades of pink are extremely good

colours with which to create your dog's personal space. These hues also encourage its own personal energies to develop, essential for a happy and healthy dog.

Having transformed the colour and look of your home, open all the windows and allow as much fresh air in as possible. Burn some pleasant incense in all the rooms, as this creates a beautiful, well-balanced atmosphere. Try to persuade your dog to wander around the house, from room to room, noting its reaction to each one. This will give you some indication as to the success of your transformation. A well-balanced atmosphere in the home creates a well-balanced family. Dogs and cats help to facilitate a warm and pleasant atmosphere, and should there be anything untoward in the house they will be the first to know it. Should your dog appear restless or agitated in a particular part of the house, you can then rest assured that the atmosphere there is not balanced and the problem needs to be addressed as soon as possible.

When a home has a harmonious atmosphere it will always be reflected in the general demeanour of your dog or cat. In fact, your pet's happiness and well-being is always a good indication that you are living in a house with a healthy and happy atmosphere.

When moving into a new home you will always see your dog or cat roaming from room to room, almost as though it is looking for someone. Dogs and cats are curious creatures, whose senses are extremely acute, and always finely attuned to the subtle energies of the surrounding atmosphere. If there is anything whatsoever amiss in your home your pet will most certainly know about it.

As I have said in a previous chapter, because of your pet's sensitivity towards the vibrations of colour you can use colour to encourage it to get well when it is a little under the weather. Surrounding your pet with the appropriate colours can uplift it when energy is lacking, or calm it down when it is boisterous and energetic. In fact, colour has an amazing effect on the psyche and not just at a subconscious level either. Even wrapping your pet in a *blue* blanket encourages the healing process when it is not well. When your pet is suffering the effects of a severe chill, a *red* blanket will encourage warmth and help to alleviate the symptoms. *Pink* is an ideal colour for calming your pet, particularly when it has been traumatised, or even when it is recovering from surgery. *Green* is traditionally the colour associated with harmony, and may be used for heart conditions. Take care not to surround your hyperactive pet with too much *yellow;* this colour will stimulate it and probably make it even more hyperactive. However, yellow may be used when your pet is constipated or suffering with bladder or kidney problems. When using *yellow* it should always be accompanied by another less aggressive colour to defuse it a little, such as *blue. Purple* or *violet* is an excellent all-round tonic and will have a holistic effect on your dog or cats body. It will calm it down and sooth away any pain, and will also encourage the restoration of depleted energy reserves.

A well balanced colour arrangement around the home encourages harmony and promotes health and happiness within the whole family. A happy home makes a happy and healthy pet.

CHAPTER TWENTY-ONE

YOUR PET'S AURA

With today's scientific advancements there is very little that cannot be achieved with modern technology. Science has already taken man to the moon and to mars, and will no doubt conquer new frontiers of space in the not too distant future. Because of the remarkable scientific breakthroughs man is no longer confined to the limitations once imposed upon him by the natural laws of the planet upon which we live; because of science anything is now possible. Amongst all of man's incredible technological achievements the more subtle aspects of man's being can now be photographed in full colour, giving incredible insights into the spiritual, emotional and physical sides of the human nature. I am of course referring to the human aura – a vaporous mass of electro-magnetic particles surrounding every living thing. The majority of people use the word 'aura' to describe the ambience of a house or person, saying 'This house has an aura of peace', or 'He has an aura of calm and serenity about him.' Today though the aura is far more than just a descriptive term – it is now a scientific fact as well as a metaphysical phenomenon. Today integrated into so called 'New Age' terminology the word aura can be found as a mystical phenomenon and an essential part of man's spiritual nature. Although the metaphysical interpretations of the aura cannot be disputed, today it can also be scientifically explored giving a much more clearly defined analysis of man's health and well being.

Husband and wife team, Semyon and Valentina Kirlian from Krasnodar near the Black Sea, were in fact the first to develop a camera to photograph the aura. Although an extremely crude apparatus, the monochrome photographs it produced made visible the auric emanations from the hands. It was the Kirlian's belief that disease was apparent in the aura long before it manifested in the physical body. The camera was an innovation and its use as a diagnostic tool was invaluable at the time. Today however, a more elaborate and sophisticated digital camera has been developed which allows the entire aura to be photographed in colour. Although the colours in the human aura change with every passing thought, feeling and emotion, it has been observed that a predominant part of the colourful vaporous mass surrounding the body does not change. This aspect of the aura is believed to represent the character, which of course does not change so spontaneously. Other aspects of the aura are linked to the spiritual status of the individual, the health and also the psychological nature. For example, the halo of tradition painted around the heads of saints in medieval art represented the divinity or spirituality of the individual depicted in the paintings. In fact, the golden light around the heads of saints is sometimes seen in the aura photographs of some advanced yogi masters, or occasionally around the heads of some monastic figures who devote their lives to prayer and meditation. Whilst the auras of animals would not be expected to exhibit signs of spirituality, some startling revelations were discovered by some researching the phenomenon. Using the more up-to-date aura camera, researchers in Russia photographed the auras of several breeds of dogs and cats, and were quite amazed at the outcome of some of them. A bright light, similar to a halo, was apparent in the photographs taken of the auras of dogs that had been specially trained to care for humans, and the overall appearance was consistent with the auras of individuals with advanced spiri-tuals natures. These auric photographs were compared to others taken of dogs that had been trained to be used in the security of a large factory in Moscow, and there was a marked difference in all of them. The aura photographs of Alsatians and Rottweilers contained colours that were dull with flashes of deep red all through them, consistent with aggression and alertness.

The auras of 20 children who had been brought up with either a pet dog or cat were also photographed, and the auras of 18 out of the 20 children revealed colours that were consistent with calmness and a well-balanced emotional nature. Aquamarine and midnight blue were predominant in these aura photographs, and it was concluded that these colours were the result of living with a pet.

The bioluminescence of the aura is produced when the cells of the body convert chemical energy into light energy, culminating into an incredible luminous glow around the body. The bioluminescence shows the degree of vitality present and the level of compassion as well as the capacity to love. In photographs taken of the auras of the dogs that work with disabled people the bioluminescence was extremely bright and vibrant, indicative of the sensitivity and caring nature. The experiments were quite conclusive and proved without a doubt that dogs do have the capacity to change the lives of humans.

Herbert Neiberg, Ph.D., director of behavioural medicine at Four Winds Hospital in Pounds Ridge, New York, and the author of Pet Loss, commented, 'I don't care how good a husband, wife, mother or a father is, nobody accepts you like a pet does. Pets are the only unconditionally accepting organisms in the world.'

'I recommend pets to people who have had a loss in their lives, people who are lonely,' added Stephen Sinatra, M.D, cardiologist and bioenergetic psychotherapist, and the author of Optimum Health: 'A Natural Lifesaving Prescription for Your Mind & Body. 'Cats, dogs, even a parrot is wonderful. Sometimes I'll even recommend fish because they're easier to take care of as pets. Anytime you can use a pet with a person who feels isolated, it helps make a connection for them in the world.'

According to Alan M. Beck, PhD, director of the Centre for the Human-Animal Bond at Purdue University in West Lafayette, Indiana, 'It's a two-way street. We are so pre-wired to like animals. Ever since we started living in villages and cities, man has kept pets. They are so important to so many people. Ninety-nine percent of people talk to their dogs and cats – and the other one percent lie.'

Animals have always been featured in movies, and we have always been enthralled by their exploits and adventures. From the adventures of Lassie and the Alsatian Rin Tin Tin right up to Mr Ed the talking horse, animals have always helped us to escape reality and to live for a time in a world of fantasy and make-believe. The idea that animals can talk and hold conversations with us has always fascinated us, which is probably why writers such as Beatrix Potter and others exploited animals in this way to the full. Animals do contribute something very special to our lives and help us to escape from the stresses and worries of our lives if only for a short while.

After a serious back injury, Maggie North of Vancouver was confined to the home. She calls her 4-year-old mixed shepherd, Alex, her best friend. He supports Maggie so she can stand up, ensuring that she remains stable and does not fall. Alex is also an expert at picking up dropped objects. 'He has given me independence, and I couldn't get along without him,' commented Maggie.

Multiple sclerosis sufferer, Joanne Hone, of Ontario, got her foot caught in her motorised scooter, and lay their trapped with her broken foot. Unable to move, and in a lot of pain, she called out to her dog, Kelah, a giant schnauzer who immediately brought her a cordless phone so that she call for help. Thanks to Kelah within 10 minutes Joanne received the help she needed.

There is no doubt that people would go to the doctor less frequently if they had a dog or a cat. Animals most certainly have an impact on many aspects of our physical health. 'We have known intuitively or heard anecdotally for a long time that pets' loving is life-enhancing, but now the research is starting to pour in,' said Marty Becker, a veterinarian in Twin Falls, Idaho, USA.

'People recover faster from illness when they share their lives with a pet.'

It has been found that the survival rates of patients hospitalised with coronary artery disease are dramatically higher for those who have pets – even higher than those who have the support from a spouse or their family. This is according to a survey conducted by the University of California, Davis, School of Veterinary Medicine. The facts are there, your pet has the power to heal you.

CHAPTER TWENTY-TWO

CROSS MY PAW WITH SILVER

Dogs and cats are far more in tune with the future than we humans. We spend much of our time reminiscing about the past and remembering 'the good old times'. In other words, we are used to looking back as opposed to looking forward.

Time, it would seem, is a mystery to man. Our ephemeral minds somehow have great difficulty in comprehending the true concept – that time is the greatest of all illusions. In fact, the only way in which man can actually understand time is by compartmentalising the events of his life into a *Past, Present* and *Future*.

Animals do not have this problem, for they do not have any real experiences or major events to relate to. They appear to be much more relaxed about time, living perpetually in one eternal *now*.

They seem to be able to glimpse the future at any time they want, and what exactly they perceive of their future is already present to them in their *now*.

The Animal Kingdom appears to have no problem at all dipping mentally into the great vortex of time, where the Past, Present and Future exist as one.

This ability is in fact the fundamental principle that underlies and controls the gift possessed by mystics and many psychics. Animals though have always possessed this ability, and it is partly this that enables them to sense danger when it is still far away and which also allows the dog or cat to know exactly when its owner is on the way home. This probably sounds all too metaphysical to you and it is probably not something you expected to read in a book about the healing powers of animals. However, although we have always suspected that animals possessed some sort of 'psychic' ability, it is really only in recent years that research has been done to confirm this suspicion. This is the very reason why I decided to include it in this book, and I really do feel that it is an integral part of the power our pets have over us.

If dogs and cats were able to speak our language, or perhaps if we could learn to speak theirs, we would realise that, in theory, they possess the ability to foretell our future. In fact, the very thought of walking into a fairground fortune teller's booth, to be greeted by an Old English Sheepdog, or perhaps a Labrador sitting quietly gazing into a crystal ball, waiting to tell our fortune, is certainly not as ridiculous as it sounds, not to me anyway. 'How ridiculous!' I can almost hear you say. Nonetheless, if you would allow me to indulge myself just for a little while longer, and then if you still feel the same, feel free to dismiss this chapter as nonsense. I am quite certain that our pets are already looking into our futures; although what they see there they wisely keep to themselves.

Let us suppose that these powers could be exploited by us, and that having learned to communicate with them, our pets were able to advise us of emotional, business and even health matters pertaining to our future.

It seems to be fairly easy to train our dogs to do specific tasks, so why not train them to use their psychic powers to our advantage? Your Spaniel might tell you to sell the car now before the mechanical problems start to happen in two months time. Your Labrador might advise you on future business transactions, or your Afghan Hound might tell you to get a health check-up, or not to take a holiday to a particular country next month. After all, if dogs and cats can monitor molecular changes in the atmos-phere to give an early warning about the approach of a volcanic eruption, up to 24 hours before it actually happens, then why shouldn't they be able to provide us with other information about the future? It makes sense, don't you think? You may smile, but this, I am quite certain, is what will happen in the future. The more animals are encouraged to interact with humans, the more they will evolve a sensitivity towards us, and the ability to communicate with us. I am quite sure that animals are just biding their time before they reveal all! In fact, a dog talking is not as ridiculous as it sounds. Some species of dogs appear to be so intelligent that it is quite clear that their evolutionary processes will eventually develop in them the faculties to communicate enabling them to speak.

Although most dog and cat lovers talk to their pets, in the future our pets will be able to talk back and hold long conversations with us and we with them. As animal lovers surely you can see this coming? In fact, the possibilities are endless. Imagine your dog or cat telling you exactly what kind of day it has had, and asking you what your day has been like. This surely must happen, considering the way in which a lot of domestic animals are evolving. Imagine your dog having an argument with you because it did not want to be placed in kennels while you went on your annual holiday, or perhaps disagreeing with you about your intense dislike of the dog next door. Imagine your dog shouting at you, *'How many times have I told you not to buy that brand of dog food?'*

Dogs are already halfway to being little people. Were they to develop the ability to speak, I am quite sure they would have a lot to say. Imagine what it would be like in the future if dogs were able to speak for themselves. What a different world it would then be if our pets could speak. There might even be dog rallies and hundreds of dogs gathering to petition 10 Downing Street, all chanting *'Give dogs the vote! Give dogs the vote!'* Maybe that's taking the idea a little too far – or is it?

However, I'm quite certain that if they could speak our language they would certainly tell us what they know of our future, and would put their psychic skills to good use, perhaps to help mankind, and to restore peace on the planet. But then, why should they when we have been so cruel to the Animal Kingdom?

Some dogs have only a superficial control over their psychic abilities, whilst others are able to use them all the time. This difference in ability I believe depends largely upon your dog's temperament, and is greatly influenced by the way he or she is treated in the family.

As with people some dogs are thinkers, whilst others appear to have butterfly minds and have great difficulty in concentrating on anything for any length of time. The thinking dog is usually the most psychic. This creature needs a great deal of stimulation and appreciates its master speaking to it whenever possible. It also loves music. It is a very intelligent dog, and possesses a great capacity to learn, and to learn very quickly. Also, watch how its gaze often moves around the room, as though seeing something you cannot. Ok, it may well be just watching a fly or some other insect; but humour me for a moment. Your dog or cat very often sees things you cannot.

The canine and feline worlds are certainly much more in tune with the more subtle energies of the universe than we are, and they can therefore see, hear and sense far more than we can. A dog or cat is nearly always the first to sense an unpleasant atmosphere, even when we are totally oblivious to it. They are always fully aware of those who do not like them, and just as aware of those who do.

Take a look at a dog who is loved and cared for, as opposed to the one who is not. Love encourages a dog to almost shine, not just psychically speaking, but in every way possible. The eyes of an unloved dog are dull and almost cry out for love. Its auric bioluminescence is dull and lifeless, and it emits such a strong sense of sadness, that anyone with a degree of sensitivity could not fail to see it.

Animals ask for nothing other than to be loved. They know full well that is exactly why they are here on this planet – to love and to be loved. Maybe in the future dogs and cats will have evolved so much that before they come to live with us we will need to first be interviewed by them to see if we are suitable. Then, if we do not meet all the criteria they will say, 'Thanks, but no thanks!'

Maybe the future will see an animal revolution, and perhaps then we will have to pay our pets for their services. Then, I am quite sure they will say, 'Cross my paw with silver.'

CHAPTER TWENTY-THREE

ESP AND HORSES

I suppose that any book giving the scientific as well as the metaphysical facts of animals must even today be considered quite controversial, and although written with a serious approach to the subject of the healing powers of animals, to the sceptic the whole subject becomes a little suspect when the words 'psychic' or 'extra-sensory perception are seen to be used. Nonetheless, even serious researchers of the subject of extra-sensory abilities in animals are becoming more and more convinced that such metaphysical skills do exist. Although it was my intention to primarily explore the innumerable possibilities of dogs and cats, within the last six years or so I have been fortunate to live in a very horse orientated community in which I have been privileged to come into close proximity with more than one of these magnificent creatures. As a small child, because of sickness I spent most of my days either in hospital or at home in bed. In both places I was visited by Blossom an elderly white horse owned by a friend of my father. They would bring the horse to the nearby baby hospital where I would be in my cot on the veranda in the open air. Blossom would always seem as excited to see me as I was to see her, and she would demonstrate this by reaching over to lick my face and allow me to cuddle her. Even at home the downstairs window would be opened wide to allow Blossom to poke her head in to lick my face all over. Thinking back to those early years I can still recall the way Blossom made me feel on each of her visits, happy and full of excitement and energy. Knowing what I now know I am quite certain there was more taking place then than just mere physical contact with the gentle horse. I have explained in a previous chapter that seventeen century monks would encourage the patients at their monastic asylum to ride horses round and round in a circle, in the belief that this would lift their spirits and help to calm them down. The monks also encouraged the patients to embrace the horses, a further therapeutic process to calm their tormented minds.

As any horse lover will affirm horses are without a doubt one of the most extraordinary creatures on this planet. They are powerful and yet very graceful and always possess an air of dignity. Just standing close to a horse is sufficient to feel its incredible energy. Looking into the eyes of these creatures one gets the sense that something far greater than a horse is looking out at you, reaching out to you from another world – perhaps even from another time.

Henry Blake, a horse expert was brought an Arab-cross Welsh six-year-old for 'gentling', as it is referred to, a process whereby a horse with an abundance of excitable and anxious energy is calmed down by gently talking to it, before stroking it softly with the fingertips. Having built a strong and trusting relationship with the horse after working with it for at least three months, he allowed a friend of the family to take it for a ride. She herself was a horse owner and an extremely competent rider and so he had no worries about her taking it for a trot. Within half an hour Henry Blake felt his stomach muscles tighten and he was suddenly overwhelmed with feelings of anxiety and apprehension. He just knew that he was receiving these feelings from the horse and felt there must be something wrong. He jumped in his car and accompanied by his son went looking for them. The woman and the horse were at least two miles away and to all intents and purposes looking very much like there was a problem. His suspicions had been correct. The cross-breed horse was distressed and very agitated and obviously not pleased. Henry calmed the creature down in no time and helped his friend to dismount. He then allowed his son, who was also a competent rider, to take the horse back to the stables, seemingly with no problems at all. A couple of days later Henry allowed another friend to take the horse for a gallop, and once again he felt his stomach muscles tighten accompanied by feelings of anxiety and apprehension. Following his instinct as before, he again found the horse in a distressed state and rearing up on its hind legs. This time it took a little longer to calm it down, but he was now in no doubt that he had received telepathic signals from the horse who had grown to trust him. As a well respected horse expert, Henry Blake knew that by making his discovery public he might compromise his professional integrity and most probably be ridiculed by his peers. Nonetheless, he voiced his strong beliefs in the phenomenon of extra-sensory perception, and even made it known that he knew when there was something wrong with a horse. Henry Blake claimed to be able to receive communication from horses primarily through the phenomenon of telepathy. His interest in the whole process of mind-to-mind communication led him to research it further. He had always been a heavy sleeper, but was woken up one night with strong feelings that something was wrong with one of his horses. However, upon investigation he found to his surprise that it wasn't a horse but a cow who was distressed. The cow was calving but with a breech delivery and her obvious difficulty had somehow been transmitted to Henry. He required no further evidence that animals were somehow able to transmit their feelings to him. He was convinced that extra-sensory perception was a fact and that he could 'feel' the moods of animals without actually seeing or hearing them. He was in no doubt that the information conveyed to him was received outside the range of the normal five senses, and required no further convincing that all animals used this process with great ease. Henry Blake's investigations into extra-sensory perception in animals led him to conclude that all animals are able to use this faculty in some way to convey their moods, emotions and certain 'limited ideas'. This process of communication combined with those of sounds and signs used by the animal, somehow compared with the manner and general ways in which humans convey their thoughts and feelings through the process of speech. He further claimed that when a horse is either excited or feeling under the weather that these emotions are transmitted directly to us and that when we are depressed and not feeling too well, horses can feel it too. Henry Blake had to admit that his research and theories on extra-sensory perception were quite controversial particularly in the eyes of the academic world, who would probably view animal communication with disdain and scepticism. Nonetheless, he was convinced that the process of e.s.p was nearly always used by animals to convey their feelings and moods to humans and to other animals. Henry Blake was also convinced that physical sensations such as hunger, thirst and pain are also conveyed by animals through the phenomenon of telepathy, and that most good vets most definitely have the capacity to receive such signals.

Living in a farming community as I do, I have spoken to numerous horse owners about how their horse conveys its feeling to them, and they all agree that they just 'know' what their horse wants and exactly how it feels. This sort of telepathic relationship is fairly typical amongst horse owners who all seem to have an extremely strong 'psychic' connection with their horses. In fact, it is a general consensus of opinion that of all the Animal Kingdom horses seem to be the most telepathic and more able than any other animal to transmit their thoughts to humans. Not being a horse owner I can't really dispute this claim, but what I am sure of is the healing vibrations horses most definitely transmit to humans, without any great effort at all. Although the title of this book, *A WAG'S AS GOOD AS A SMILE* may not be applied to horses, the healing abilities of these incredible creatures do exist without any question at all.

CHAPTER TWENTY-FOUR

PET POWER

I am quite certain that a book of this nature will be completely dismissed as nonsense by those who simply do not like animals. However, I cannot even begin to imagine why anyone could dislike those creatures that have played such an important part in our lives from time immemorial. In fact, my father used to say 'Anyone who doesn't like animals does not like people!' As a child I could never understand the logic in this statement, but today knowing what I know about animals and the amazing way they affect us I fully understand what he meant. People who say that they 'hate' animals I am sure today are in a minority. Nonetheless, on one occasion a visitor to my home grimaced at the very sight of our pussycat, Pesi (now deceased) pleading with us to take her into another room. 'I hate cats!' The woman announced disdainfully, 'I can't stand them!' I must say that not only were my wife and I quite surprised with her attitude, we were also both extremely offended to think that we had welcomed her into our home only to have our cat, Pesi, insulted in this way. Needless to say, she is no longer a friend and was most certainly not invited again. The sad thing about that experience was she did not seem to know she had done anything wrong. Although not all people who dislike animals express their displeasure so rudely, one can always tell when a person is not so keen. He or she never attempts to stroke a cat or dog, and will never reciprocate when the creature proffers a paw or cuddles up to them. But you've probably noticed that your cat or dog just knows when visitors to your home are not too keen on them. Initially a dog will make an effort to win the person over by trying to at least instigate some form of contact. However, a dog's patience is very limited and it will only try for a short while before abandoning the attempt. Cats are quite cunning and do have a completely different strategy to dogs. In fact, they possess a power that is not in any way possessed by dogs. They are persistent and will try everything to encourage the visitor to make some effort to stroke them. The cat will target the person's legs first of all, weaving in and out in a figure eight shape. If this carefully planned manoeuvre has not done the job of encouraging even a little stroke, then plan two will come into action. The cat will then rub against the back of the person's legs, ensuring that its personal fragrance is evenly deposited all over them. If this doesn't work the person usually feels safer sitting down. This is probably the worst move they could have made, and almost certainly a part of the cat's cunning plan. The lap is then targeted and the game is over. Once in position, the cat snuggles down and at this point the family visitor usually submits. Although he or she may not leave the house as a fully fledged cat-lover, of one thing you can rest assured and that is that their attitude to cats will never, ever be the same again. They may not admit it right away, but their cat-hating days are over.

Both cats and dogs are without a doubt the philosophers of the family. Although you may not always be aware of it their in-built mental radar system is constantly scanning its surrounding environment, monitoring molecular changes in the atmosphere, always on the lookout for intruders of one kind or another. Your pet is in fact your own personal security guard and is capable of processing data from the unseen environment as well as the visible. Both dogs and cats are capable of detecting unfamiliar fragrances, personal odours of strangers to the home at great distances. Even when they appear to be asleep their antennae is in constant operation, noting every sound and slightest movement, alert and ready to sound the alarm. Our pets are amazing creatures really and I don't know what we would do without them. Their senses are so acute that they can distinguish their owner's footsteps from those of a stranger, and even recognise him or her by personal smell. Little wonder then that we sometimes see them suddenly sit up to look at something that's not there. There is no question about it that our pets are quite psychically attuned to the nature of things, and never fail to encourage and reassure us when we are feeling a little depressed or just under the weather. Animal lovers do develop a natural and very strong psychic bond with their pets, which nearly always transcends the confines of speech. As any lover of animals will affirm some form of mental dialogue does take place between them and their dog or cat, and each understands perfectly well what the other is saying. A person who lives alone never feels lonely when they have the company of a dog or cat, and the dog who looks after its disabled owner is always looked upon as a 'good friend' and never just a pet. With all the love and encouragement given to us by our pets, there is little wonder we feel so helpless when they are not too well! Although not a substitute for a visit to the vet, crystals are a gentle way of encouraging balance in your pet's energy system and for maintaining its levels of vitality when it is recovering from illness. For this reason I have listed some of the most powerful crystals and explained how they can be used to help your pet.

CRYSTAL POWER FOR ANIMALS

Although Crystal Healing methods are not what the majority of people would choose as a form of treatment for their pet, they are nonetheless used by many people with some success. In fact, Crystal therapy is by no means a new concept and was a method employed by the ancient Egyptians to heal the bodies and the minds of both animals and people. I must say though that the ancient Egyptians carried Crystal Therapy to the extreme, as the practitioners of this method of healing used to crush the crystals into a fine powder to be taken orally by the patient. This method is most certainly not recommended though, as more patients died than were actually cured, probably as a direct consequence of the treatment used.

Because dogs and cats can quite easily monitor molecular changes in the atmosphere, they can somehow 'home-in' to crystal energy with great ease. For this reason alone, our pets respond very quickly to the healing properties of crystals, and it is a healing therapy that should be used to complement traditional medicine and **NOT** as a substitute for it.

Working on the premise that all crystals produce different energies, and vibrate at varying frequencies, each individual crystal then will understandably have an effect on a specific illness. However, before the appropriate crystal can be selected you must have a little understanding of the healing properties of the various crystals you are going to use.

ROSE QUARTZ: This is usually described as the emotional stone. The Rose Quartz is in fact extremely effective when treating any condition affecting the emotions. Should your pet be extremely nervous or perhaps recovering from the loss of a litter or a mate, simply surround it with several pieces of Rose Quartz strategically placed around your pet's bed, and you should see some improvement in a very short time. The Rose Quartz is also extremely effective when your little creature is recovering from a serious illness. It aids the process of recovery and, when combined with other crystals (mentioned elsewhere) it is a powerful healing tool.

AMETHYST: Most probably because of the beautiful deep purple colour of the Amethyst it is often referred to as the 'Spiritual Stone.' This has to be one of the most powerful healing crystals and is effective in the healing of almost any illness, regardless of the severity. Amethyst is very effective in the treatment of pain, particularly when it is associated with cancer or other related conditions. Because of Amethyst's calming effect upon the mind, it is extremely effective in the treatment of anxiety. Should you live with an over-anxious or nervous pet, apply the same procedure as suggested with the Rose Quartz and improvement should be almost instantaneous. In fact, the Amethyst stone can be used as a 'Tonic' for your pet, and by simply placing a piece under its bed, particularly in the area of his or her head, your little creature should wake up feeling much more chilled out, so to speak. The Amethyst can also be used to revitalise the more mature pet. Combined with Rose Quartz, Amethyst will help to sustain the life of an elderly pet, particularly when his or her mobility has been greatly impaired.

CLEAR QUARTZ: This magnificent crystal enhances the energy in anything else placed close to it. Because it is able to retain Universal Energy, simply by placing it next to your pet when he or she is asleep will suffice to increase the creature's own self-healing. In fact, the clear Quartz is an ideal tonic for the elderly pet, and you should not be surprised to see your dog or cat suddenly discover a whole new lease of life when treated with it. The clear Quartz can in fact be used as a complementary tool combined with other crystals. Even when placed strategically around the home the clear Quartz has a detoxing effect upon the atmosphere. Combined with Amethyst it will transform a tense, uneasy atmosphere into a more relaxed and serene one.

LAPIS LAZULI: This is perhaps one of those stones that has a multitude of uses. It was used by the ancients to bring good luck and protection in battle. Whilst it has a wonderful healing effect upon the whole body, it is particularly effective in the treatment of throat conditions. Should your little creature be quite timid and lacking in confidence, Lapis Lazuli will boost his or her morale. The ears and throat areas are greatly affected by this beautiful stone and, its calming blue hue will promote equilibrium of both the body and the mind.

YELLOW CITRINE: Although not as popular as Amethyst, Rose Quartz and Clear Quartz, Yellow Citrine has a remarkable healing effect upon the nervous system and stomach areas. This stone is in fact greatly underestimated and may be combined with Carnelian to alleviate either gynaecological disorders in the female animal or prostate problems in the male. Yellow Citrine may also have a stimulating effect upon the bladder and kidneys and will encourage healing in these areas when combined with Amethyst.

TIGER'S EYE: The healing properties of the Tiger's Eye are perhaps dismissed too quickly, as the majority of people only look upon this stone as something that looks nice in a ring or perhaps a pendant. However, the Tiger's Eye is quite a versatile stone and possesses numerous healing properties. It is particularly useful in the treatment of conditions which affect the head, especially in the more mature creature. It sometimes has a stimulating effect upon the brain and can make an elderly animal more alert.

SNOWFLAKE OBSIDIAN: The healing properties of this stone are also greatly underestimated as it does not appear to be as popular as most of the others. The ancient Egyptians used to grind the Snowflake Obsidian into a fine powder and use it as a medicine to treat any condition that caused loss of memory. It encourages a sick and lethargic creature to be more lively and aware and precipitates its own self-healing processes. It can be used for certain minor skin irritations also, particularly when the condition has affected the creature's psychological status.

CARNELIAN: Although not common knowledge, carnelian may be used in the treatment of gynaecological problems, particularly in the more mature creature. Although this gem produces some remarkable results when several pieces are simply placed around your pet's bed, when combined with clear quartz and amethyst its healing properties become extremely powerful.

METHODS AND TREATMENTS

Although there are numerous ways in which crystals may be used for healing, there is no one specific method that is better than the others. In fact, as with any so called *New Age* therapy it is nearly always best to follow one's instincts when using crystals and to achieve the best results experiment as much as possible. The most popular and traditional way is simply to surround your pet with the appropriate crystals whilst he or she is resting. The method I would recommend, particularly when using a combination of crystals in the treatment, is to place them alternately around your pet at strategic points. This is best done when your pet is asleep as then the healing emanations are given the opportunity to be established. The crystals can be sown into your pet's bed or you can make a special crystal cushion, making quite certain of course that they are covered with a soft padding to ensure the hard stones do not cause any discomfort to your little creature. It is immaterial whether you believe in crystal healing or not as the results are not dependent upon belief or faith.

Another favourite method with some people is to have a small piece of crystal sewn into their pet's collar. In fact, the boisterous dog would benefit from having a piece of Rose quartz or even Amethyst sewn discreetly into its collar. The effect is quite remarkable and results are nearly always seen immediately. Once the crystal's energies have been fully absorbed by your pet the colour of the crystal will fade and appear more anaemic. In fact, this is a good indication that its energies of been fully discharged.

I have listed the above Crystal healing properties purely as guidelines to help you find the correct crystal for your pet's condition. However, it is always a good idea to be guided by your instincts when choosing the appropriate crystal for your dog or cat. Nobody knows your little creature as well as you and so your love will guide you to the right healing vibrations regardless of whether or not it fits into the correct healing criteria.

CHAPTER TWENTY-FIVE

MORE FURRY TAILS

EVERYBODY'S ANGEL

The little tap on the door always told my mother that Winnie, (real name Winston) the wire haired terrier was there, waiting to come in from the cold. In fact, although this extremely friendly dog was called Winnie, (the inscription on the collar said so,) this incredibly gentle old soul was a male and most certainly not what his name suggested. He first introduced himself to my mother, one night when she was taking Lucky for his evening constitutional. From then on he became a regular caller to our house. Although we then thought that Winnie was a stray, and probably lived in one of the derelict houses nearby, he would occasionally turn up at our front door looking quite clean, as though he had been bathed.

Whenever it was raining, snowing or very windy, we could always be certain of a visit from Winnie. My mother would feed him, and then he would spend an hour in front of the fire before asking for the front door to be opened for him.

Winnie's visits to our house continued for at least three years, and to be quite honest, it never occurred to us that he visited other houses in the neighbourhood. Then suddenly Winnie stopped calling. My mother became so concerned that she went looking for him in all the places she thought he may have been, but Winnie was nowhere to be found. Then, one afternoon an envelope came through the front door. It was a thank you card from a nearby Asian family, thanking us for our kindness to Winnie who, had sadly passed away with pneumonia. In fact, we were all deeply saddened by Winnie's death. He was a character and had become a friend to our dog Lucky. It wasn't until my mother was talking to another neighbour that she discovered she too had received a similar card. In fact, nearly everyone in the street had received a thank you card through their front doors. Although my mother had thought that ours was the only house Winnie had visited, he had been a regular visitor to everyone in the street who had a dog. Good old Winnie.

THE DOG IN THE TRENCHES

The Second World War was supposed to have been 'THE WAR TO END ALL WARS'. In fact, the 1914-18 war was a cruel war to both humans and animals. Horses and donkeys were used in the trenches, and when rations were low they were slaughtered for their meat. Pigeons were also used to send messages to the mainland, and even these frequently ended up as delicacies on the officer's table. Even though animals have always been cruelly exploited, they have still remained loyal to their human friends. A fine example of this loyalty is the story of Jip, the angel of the trenches. Jip was a long haired Jack Russell who would often appear in the trenches in times of great need. Although it never occurred to the soldiers who saw him that he was a spirit dog, even though his little form shone through the darkness, his appearances were always attributed to Divine intervention. It was Private Charlie McShay who named the little dog 'Jip,' after the Jack Russell he had had as a child. Nonetheless, the wiry little dog always responded to Jip, and on one occasion even appeared when two wounded soldiers called out to him when they were trying to find their way through the trenches and back to their platoon. Jip was a hero and helped hundreds of soldiers in the trenches. It was the last week of the war when the whole mystery of Jip was solved. After leading five young soldiers through the dark and mud sodden trenches, Jip disappeared into nothingness before their very eyes. The story quickly spread that Jip was a spirit dog, and became known as *the little angel without wings.*

TAMMY'S LOVE KNOWS NO BOUNDS

10-year-old Nicky Taylor and his beautiful Persian cat, Tammy, were inseparable. Tammy often followed Nicky to school, and always waited patiently at the front door of their home for his return. Tammy slept on Nicky's bed, ate her meals with him and even played with him. Everyone was agreed, Tammy and Nicky were very special friends, and if there were such things as soul mates, then they most definitely were.

Although in the winter months Tammy was kept indoors, one very cold and frosty morning in December she slipped through an open door. Tammy had no sooner reached the road when she was hit by a delivery van. Sadly, the beautiful Persian pussycat was killed outright. Nicky was devastated and inconsolable. His parents did not know what to do. Their son would not eat or play out, and every night they would listen to him sobbing in his bedroom.

Three weeks had passed by and Nicky was still fretting. His parents seriously considered buying a replacement for Tammy, but the very suggestion made their son hysterical. Although Nicky gradually showed signs of improvement, it was quite clear to his parents that he still missed his pussycat terribly. The situation became more serious when Nicky's father announced that a new position at work meant that the family would be moving to Canada for a year. Nicky was inconsolable. He did not want to move from the house in which he had lived with his friend Tammy. The little boy somehow believed that by moving to another country Tammy would wonder where they had gone. Even though his mother tried to console him, her efforts were in vain and her son was just not convinced.

Within four weeks they had moved to Canada. As it was only for one year, the Taylor's had let their house through a local estate agent. Even this did not pacify Nicky who simply wanted desperately to stay at home.

Nicky's parents thought that their son would settle down

once they had arrived in their new home. At least in Canada there was such a lot for a young boy to do, but still Nicky was sad and very depressed and showed no interest in anything. His parents could not understand why he didn't show any signs of improvement, and were even considering returning to England.

There was nothing else for it, the Taylor's decided, their son was more important. Without telling Nicky, his parents decided to leave Canada and return to their home in the United Kingdom. Then, suddenly, Nicky showed signs of recovery. He seemed to become his old self again, and began showing an interest in the activities of the other children in the vicinity. Although extremely pleased, the Taylors were somewhat puzzled. They did not have to leave Canada at all.

Going to check on her son before going to bed one night, Nicky's mother could hear him talking to someone. As she thought he was talking in his sleep, she listened for a moment outside his door before quietly opening it. Nicky was sitting bolt upright in bed. 'It's alright mummy,' he smiled broadly. 'Tammy's gone now.'

'What do you mean?' she answered curiously, turning on the light.

'I didn't tell you, but Tammy comes to see me every night.'

Nicky's mother felt a chill pass through her. She sat on the edge of his bed and watched him snuggle contentedly down beneath the duvet. Reaching over to kiss him goodnight, she noticed cat fur all over the duvet. 'What's this?' asked his mother, not prepared for her son's answer.

'I've just told you, mummy,' Nicky replied tiredly. 'Tammy comes to see me every night. She's alright now and wants me to be happy.' Nicky fell into a deep sleep. His mother turned off the light and sat on Nicky's bed for a few moments thinking about what her son had said. Just as she was about to leave the room she heard the unmistakable sound of Tammy meowing. She felt the same chill pass through her body, and then a smile broke across her lips. She knew now that her son would be alright, Tammy had come back to make sure. Tammy's love truly knows no bounds.

THE CHURCH GOING DOG

Barbara Jones had had Ben, her little brown and white mongrel dog, since he was six weeks old. He was now fifteen and showing signs of old age. Barbara had noticed just how much Ben had slowed down over the last six months and was dreading the day when she would lose him. He was one of the family and her children loved him. Ben was allowed to come and go as he pleased, and over the years had become quite a personality in the neighbourhood. In fact, everybody knew Ben, who could often be seen playing with the children, either on the corner of the street, or on the playground of St Martin's school. Barbara always knew where Ben was and he very rarely strayed very far. Her dog was a creature of habit and always knew exactly when it was time to be fed. However, things suddenly changed one late afternoon when, to Barbara's surprise, Ben failed to come home as he always did at 5pm prompt. She searched the streets frantically, praying that nothing had happened to him. After she had exhausted all Ben's favourite places, she decided that it was best to return home. As she began making her way towards her front door, she heard someone call her from across the street. 'Are you looking for Ben?' her neighbour asked. 'Only I've just seen him in the church.'

'In the church?' replied Barbara, somewhat puzzled. 'Which church?'

'St Martin's,' smiled the woman. 'On Stapleton Avenue. Do you know where that is?'

'Yes, I know where it is.' She said quickly. This was her church and also the church in which she had been married. 'How strange!' Barbara thought, knowing full well that Ben did not know that, how could he.

As St Martin's was quite a distance from where she lived, Barbara decided to drive there. This would also make it easier to get Ben home. Sure enough, just as her neighbour had said, Ben was in the church, lying in the centre aisle in front of the altar rail. As soon as she called her dog he immediately ran to her wagging his tail.

Thinking that it was just a one-off coincidence, Barbara thought no more about her dog's visit to the church. It wasn't till he went missing again three days later. Just as before she found Ben in St Martin's church, lying in exactly the same place in front of the altar rail. This time, however, she began to think there was more to it. In fact, this became a regular occurrence every two or three days. Barbara became so used to it that she just left him to return home by himself.

Four months went by, and sadly, Ben suddenly died of heart failure. Although they knew it had to come one day, Barbara and her family were heartbroken. She couldn't help but think of Ben's visits to the church and wondered why he had chosen that particular one. Then, one day she had a visit from St Martin's priest, Father McGillin.

'I heard about your dog Ben,' he said sympathetically. 'I know you're not in my parish, but...' he paused.

Even though Barbara was no longer in St Martin's parish, she had been Christened there and it was where she married her husband Phil. But how did the priest know her dog's name? She looked at him curiously.

'Ben often visited my church,' he continued. 'He would just lie in front of the altar. I would swear, to all intents and purposes that he was praying.'

'Praying?' retorted Barbara with surprise at what she was hearing. 'Praying?'

'Yes, praying!' He replied, a serious look on his face. 'The cleaner first saw him and was all set to chase him into the street. But then she noticed the look in his eyes.'

'Look?' she said. 'What do you mean?'

'I can't really explain. She called me to take a look at him and he just looked so peaceful. We decided he was doing no harm. But then he returned a few days later and sat in exactly the same place in front of the altar rail. He often came. I thought he was a stray and took a look at his collar. That's how I knew his name.'

'Oh, I see,' answered Barbara. 'Thank you for letting me know.'

'He was quite a special dog, I'm sure of that.'

'I know,' said Barbara sadly, a tear showing in the corner of her eye. 'He was very special.'

CHAPTER TWENTY-SIX

HOMOEOPATHIC WAYS TO TREAT YOUR PET

Over the last thirty years or so the interest in homoeopathy as a safe way to treat all manner of illnesses has grown throughout the world. Although thousands of people all over the world use homoeopathic preparations as an alternative to allopathic treatments it must never be used as a substitute for conventional medicine, but simply to complement it.

Although homoeopathy as we know it today was evolved in the latter part of the 18th century, and was developed as a treatment by physician and chemist Samuel Hahnemann, it was in fact used by Hippocrates, the Greek founder of medicine, sometime around 450 BC. The Swiss alchemist, Paracelsus experimented with homoeopathic treatments primarily on the philosophy of *Like cures like.*

Homoeopathy is in fact derived from the Greek word *Homoios,* meaning 'like', and so homoeopathic preparations treat the condition using a substance that produces the symptoms of the condition as are apparent in the patient. Although those who use homoeopathy usually do have a great deal of faith in its effectiveness, homoeopathic preparations produce the same results on animals which excludes any possibility of faith playing a vital part in the treatment.

I have listed below the most popular remedies used to treat simple ailments in your pet.

HOMOEOPATHY AND YOUR PET
AGGRESSION

Belladonna may be used when your pet shows signs of

aggression, and will help to encourage a more evenly balanced temperament.

ARTHRITIS

Rhus toxicodendron (Rhus. Tox) may be administered to your pet when the arthritic condition appears to improve with a little exercise. When there is some swelling in the joints **Apis Mellifica** *(Apis Mel)* may be integrated into the treatment, and if there are signs of bruising **Arnica Montana** will encourage the healing process and alleviate the discomfort. **Calcarea Fluorica** *(Calc. Fluor)* should be introduced into the treatment when the bone shows signs of being badly affected. **Bryonia alba** *(Bryonia)* should be used if the condition appears worse when the creature exercises.

APPETITE PROBLEMS

Carbo Vegetabilis (Carbo Veg) will help to improve the appetite when your pet is suffering from a minor tummy upset. When loss of appetite is accompanied by constipation **Nux vomica** *(Nux vom)* will help. When your little creature appears to be hungry but turns his or her nose up at the dish of food **Arsenicum.Album** *(Arsen.Alb)* should help to heal the condition.

BRUISES

Arnica Montana (Arnica) will encourage the healing of minor bruises, but for the more severe bruising **Ruta graveolens** *(Ruta Grav)* will facilitate the healing process. When there is bruising with broken skin **Hamamelis virginica** *(Hamamelis)* will encourage tissue restoration and encourage healing.

COUGH

Phosphorus usually helps a dry cough. However, if the cough appears to improve when your cat or dog is resting then **Bryonia Alba** *(Bryonia)* should bring relief. If the cough appears dry and spasmodic, **Cuprum Metalicum**. *(Cuprum Met.)* will promote healing. Should the cough cause your pet to retch **Drosera rotundifolia** *(Drosera)* will bring improvement.

CONJUNCTIVITIS

Argentum Nitricum *(Argent. Nit,)* may be administered for minor less complicated cases of conjunctivitis, which will also ease the irritation that accompanies the condition. **Pulsatilla nigricans** *(Pulsatilla)* will alleviate the condition when catarrh is involved. When the eyes have been irritated by the wind **Euphrasia officinalis** *(Euphrasia)* usually helps. When the lids are red and inflamed **Calcarea Carbonica** *(Calc. Carb.)* will bring relief.

DIARRHOEA

Arsenicum Album *(Arsen. Alb.)* may be administered when the motion is fairly loose or watery, but when the motion is extremely loose and bloodstained, **Mercurius Solubilis** *(Merc. Sol.)* should be used. When your pet is extremely nervous **Argentum Nitricum** *(Argent. Nit.)* will bring relief. When your pet appears debilitated **Cuprum Metallicum** *(Cuprum Met,)* will alleviate the condition.

EAR INFECTIONS

Hepar Sulphuris *(Hepar Sulph.)* should quickly clear an ear infection, especially when it is sensitive to the touch. When there is some discomfort accompanied by a fowl smelling discharge **Mercurius Solubilis** *(Merc, Sol.)*should be given. **Arsenicum Album** *(Arsen. Alb.)* should be administered when the skin in the external ear is dry with a slight discharge, and which appears to be worse at night.

For Chronic ear conditions **Rhus Toxicodendron**. *(Rhus. Tox.)* should be used.

EXHAUSTION

Arnica Montana (Arnica) will encourage your pet's recovery from illness and help to replenish its depleted energy levels. When the creature is exhausted perhaps following some stressful experience **Kalium Phosphoricum** *(Kali. Phos)* will encourage the restoration of its vitality.

EYELIDS

Phosphorous will help the pet whose eyelids are swollen and also when it is sensitive to sudden noise. **Rhus toxicodendron** *(Rhus tox.)* will ease the symptoms of your dog or cat's inflamed eyelids especially when the symptoms always seem worse when it rises from their bed. When catarrh causes a discharge to be apparent on the eyelids **Kalium Bichromicum** *(Kali. Bich.)* will clear the condition and encourage healing.

EYES

Euphrasia officinalis (Euphrasia) will ease the discomfort of eyes that water profusely and will help to clear the condition completely.

FRETTING OR BEREAVEMENT

Ignatia amara (Ignatia) will help your pet when they are fretting for whatever the reason, for example, when they have been boarded in kennels whilst you are on holiday. It will also promote calmness should a dog or cat be suffering from bereavement.

GASTRITIS

Phosphorus will help to settle your pet when it vomits soon after it has eaten. **Arsenicum Album** *(Arsen.Alb.)* will bring relief when the condition is accompanied by diarrhoea. When the vomiting is constantly repeated **Ipecacuanha** *(Ipecac)* will ease the discomfort.

INSOMNIA

Arsenicum Album (Arsen. Alb.) will help your elderly pet if it has difficulty sleeping.

INJURIES

Arnica Montana (Arnica) will bring about instant relief to minor injuries with extensive bruising. When the injury results in a painful strain **Ruta graveolens** *(Ruta Grav.)* will ease the discomfort.

INSECT BITES

Apis mellifica *(Apis Mel)* can relieve the discomfort of a wasp or bee sting, and **Hypericum perforatum** *(Hypericum)* will promote healing to a Horse-fly bite. In all cases though it is advisable to bath with *Pyrethrum liquid.*

NERVOUSNESS, FEAR OR TIMIDITY

Gelsemium sempervirens (Gelsemium) will help your pet if it is timid with apparent signs of nervousness. When your pet shows signs of being excessively frightened, as is the case on Bonfire Night, it would benefit from treatment with **Phosphorus.** (The dose depends on the severity of the condition)

When your pet has been traumatised and appears to be in a state of shock, **Arnica Montana** *(Arnica)* immediately followed by **Aconitum napellus** *(Aconite.)* The results are nearly almost instantaneous.

Please note: although I am not a qualified homoeopathic practitioner I have studied and used it for many years, and I founded The Thought Workshop, the North West's very first Centre for Psychic and Spiritual Studies and Alternative Therapies where homoeopathy was in fact used.

The above list is primarily to use as a guideline, and whilst homoeopathy is extremely safe to use, it is always better to consult a qualified homoeopath who will make a detailed assessment of the condition before prescribing the appropriate treatment.

CONCLUSION

Although I am not a qualified vet, my lifelong interest and love of animals was the thing that motivated me in the first place and led me to make a detailed study of the way our pets spiritually interact with us. I have been a professional medium and psychic for thirty years and have also lectured and held workshops and seminars all over the world, covering a broad spectrum of esoteric and metaphysical subjects. The concept of the healing powers of animals has always fascinated me, and the psychic observations I have made over the years of the way in which dogs and cats release this power was the primary inspiration for this book. I have done my very best to approach the subject of the *healing powers of our pets* in an unbiased and objective way and not as a psychic, and have also looked at the subject from a scientific as well as from a metaphysical point of view. In correlating all the data for this book I also decided to interject esoteric descriptions into the text, primarily to give the book a broader appeal. For example, I have described 'Prana' as a universal energy that is responsible for the maintenance of life - both animal and human - and explained that Prana is in fact the subtle agent that animals discharge for the purpose of healing. Although Prana is much more than this I thought it would give you a reasonable idea as to the mechanics of the way your pet can heal you.

Before putting the book together I interviewed over twenty veterinary surgeons all over the UK, the majority of whom believed totally in the phenomenon of animal healing, but surprisingly there was a minority who dismissed the concept as far-fetched and fanciful, to put it mildly. I can only surmise that those who did accept it as a fact were more sensitive and connected to the animals they treated than the ones who dismissed the idea as ridiculous.

In this age of science and technology more and more things

about the ways in which animals can help humans are being discovered, without, I must add, the use of vivisection and other heinous acts against these gentle creatures with whom we share our lives.

I am quite certain that there will always be the sceptically minded animal lovers who view the contents of the book with disdain and cynicism. Hopefully today these will be in the minority, and all that I would ask is that the book be read a few times before making a final judgement.

I also make no apologies for including colour and crystal power in the book, even though to some it may lessen the credibility and value of what I am endeavouring to say about animals. As both the concepts of colour and crystal power has been used from time immemorial, I thought it would be an extremely nice contrast to the scientific evidence given in the book and would definitely complement the entire subject. It was for this reason that I also included meditation methods to make a connection with your pet. In formulating the book in this way I knew there would be a chance that I would compromise my own professional integrity and be ridiculed in the process. Nonetheless, I wrote the book and sincerely hope that both the animal lover and sceptic will find something in it that will appeal and make sense to them.

Thank God that Fox Hunting has finally today been banned, allowing nature to find its own course of action to resolve its own problems.

THE HUNT

The early morning mist rises with shame
To reveal the flash of crimson coats;
No idle chatter from the hunters' lips
Can conceal the deathly smiles,
Nor magic away the guilt that is yet to come,
But even now is felt.

Excited hounds, hungry yet fed,
Filled with eagerness for the chase,
Mingle with impatient horses
Whose frozen breath disappears with the rising mist, but still
The guilt of the hunters' deathly smiles remain.
Already the blood of the hunted flows,
But only in the minds of the hunters,
As they rub the cold from their frosty hands
And don their caps with pride.

The misty sky reveals a curious sun,
Who peeps slyly, then retreats with shame,
As the signal is given and the hunt begins,
But for the hunted it is already over.
The wide-eyed the creature stares from the safety of the hedge,
But its safety is soon to be broken
By the crimson coats, and howling dogs,
Sounding horns, and horses at a gallop,
But led by the hunters' deathly smiles.

Confusion! And with hesitation,
The gentle creature surrenders.
Alas! No prisoners taken in this gruesome war,
As a curious sun peeps once again,
And the crimson coats congratulate each other
With outstretched hands; but the hunters' deathly smiles
Slowly disappear, and the crimson coats
Turn to coats of bloody shame...
...The journey home is always dark
But only in the minds of the hunters!
BILLY ROBERTS

6th Books, investigates the paranormal, supernatural, explainable or unexplainable. Titles cover everything included within parapsychology: how to, lifestyles, beliefs, myths, theories and memoir.